The Second Mouse Gets The Cheese

Overcome Obstacles and Drive Success by Learning from Others

Setting Goals | Taking Action | Building Relationships | Achieving Success

CHAD C BETZ

THE SECOND MOUSE GETS THE CHEESE

Overcome Obstacles and Drive Success by Learning from Others

Copyright @2021 Chad C Betz

Printed in the United States of America

CONTENTS

INTRODUCTION

Several decades ago, I heard the joke, "The early bird gets the worm, but the second mouse gets the cheese." This joke resonated with me because I never seemed to get the worm. I would achieve success but not reap the reward I anticipated. I used this joke as a way to lament what I perceived to be limited success.

Over time, my lamenting became a sign of hope. Do I have to be early to get the reward? If we push ourselves to succeed before being ready, we can suffer the same fate as the first mouse caught in a trap. Thankfully the trap is not fatal. If we keep trying, we can be the second mouse. We don't need to be first or young; we can succeed at any point in our lives. Having a strong desire to succeed in college, I heard about GE's management training program and wanted to apply. Before doing so, I talked to people and received some bad advice, and my application was not accepted SNAP; I was caught in the trap! In college, I received an award for my studies in economics. I met a professor for a prestigious school's graduate program at a reception but accidentally insulted him with a joke. SNAP; I was caught in the trap!

These experiences put me on a path of success that did not satisfy my needs and changed how I approached success. It wasn't until much later that I fully understood the lesson of the second mouse. Although he was not first, he could get the reward.

Picking up this book indicates that you may not be satisfied with your life. You may believe that your choices have diminished your ability to succeed. It's never too late to start thinking like the second mouse.

> *"Good judgment comes from experience; experience comes from bad judgment."*
> — DR. KERR L WHITE.

Boy, do I have a lot of experience! If you're like me, you've made mistakes in your life. You may think that you have made so many that your opportunities for success are now behind you.

We tend to forget that our mistakes can be lessons. I have made more mistakes than I care to count, some of which have set my career back years. Each mistake is a lesson with the potential to make me a better person and more prepared for success.

I have been researching how to bounce back from mistakes, using those lessons to find success. You can feel like a failure after a series of mistakes and not realize the value you have gained from this experience. Even if the lesson is simply knowing what not to do, you are already ahead of those without the experience.

The Second Mouse Philosophy provides a blueprint for recovering from and even leveraging your mistakes. You may not have been the early bird who got the worm, but you can still be the second mouse that gets the cheese!

The Second Mouse Philosophy

When I started carefully considering what success meant to me and what I needed to achieve, I saw my peers giving up on their goals daily. By reflecting on my experiences and talking to people from various backgrounds, I found that you can get comfortable not achieving your goals, and excuses become more acceptable as you get older. You worry about stability, which leads to an uncomfortable feeling about stretching yourself to achieve your goals.

Second Mouse Concept One: Your definition of success.

To achieve success, you need to go beyond traditional goal setting. The desires you are trying to achieve must be yours and should help you succeed, rather than following someone else's goals at the expense of your own.

Have you ever considered how those around you impact your goals? Have you ever thought about how you define success? If not, there is a good chance that you are following someone else's goals.

Second Mouse Concept Two: Influencers

There are so many influences on your life, with people around you constantly pushing their agendas, making it easy to confuse their goals with your own.

- Your parents have a powerful influence, starting when you are kids, continuing through adulthood.
- Your friends and the people you hang out with have a significant influence.
- Your spouse or partner and your children can impact your decision-making.

- Your boss and coworkers also have a substantial influence.

Their influences can cloud the lines between following your goals and following those projected on you by those influencers.

A person who helps those in transition between jobs told me a story of an accountant who owned a very successful practice. But, he hated going to work each day.

His parents told him that he would never have trouble getting a job if he earned a degree in accounting, so he studies and became an accountant. Their prediction was accurate, but he grew to hate accounting because he had followed someone else's vision. He was successful from the perspective of those around him, but he did not feel successful.

We are all vulnerable to these outside influences. I have worked with people who believed that work quantity was more important than quality. This belief caused them to put in many extra hours to produce mediocre results. I came from a place that valued more efficient methods to produce quantity and quality in a more reasonable time, but I felt pressure to work longer hours even though I was getting more done than my peers. My boss and coworkers' influence in this situation negatively impacted my ability to achieve my goals.

You can work hard and have plans, but if you do not grasp your definition of success and continue to work toward someone else's objectives while ignoring your own, you will find yourself feeling frustrated, tired, and bitter.

Overcoming the influencers and understanding your definition of success is your first step in the Second Mouse Process. Think about it. What does success mean to you? Are you actively pursuing that success, or are you floating on the current, hoping you get where you want to go? Are you helping someone else succeed at the expense of your success? To have a sustainably satisfying life, you need to understand what it takes to satisfy you. Your real success is tied to your definition of success.

Second Mouse Concept Three: Reflect on your choices

When considering your definition of success, you can look at your choices in a few ways.

1. **Big Goals** – Do you have goals you have always wanted to accomplish? Have you written down goals that you've just never acted on or that you're holding off for the "right time"?
2. **Maintain Lifestyle** – Do you have family obligations that need your attention? Do you have children, grandchildren, friends, or even pets that you want to spend more time with rather than spending extra time at work?
3. **New Experiences** – Do you want to travel or take classes? Do you want to expand your experiences? What new experiences do you want to try?

Cheese Box

The 20 Goals Exercise

1. Get a pen and paper and write down 20 goals that you would like to accomplish. Your list should include goals you would consider practical but also the goals you would consider crazy and everything in between. Crazy goals are those you're interested in but never really even thought you could achieve.

2. After writing down these 20 goals, prioritize them by the ones you would like most to achieve. Even if you think the goal is crazy, give it a higher priority if you really want to do it.

3. Look at your highest priority goals, and look for patterns. What themes do you see in your goals: more leisure time; starting a business; career change? That theme is the pattern you are looking for. When you identify patterns, your highest priority goals show you the path that can lead you toward success.

This exercise will guide you to find your definition of success.

My personal example: When I completed this exercise, I found that most of my goals were related to writing and teaching. One of my crazy goals was to write a book. It is not so crazy now! I spend more time writing and giving presentations, and feel so much more satisfied with my life.

Everyone around you can influence your goals. Each person is like a tugboat, and you're a ship coming into port. One set of friends might push you this way, your family might push you that way, and your coworkers can push you somewhere else.

You go back and forth, and if you allow the wrong "tugboat to guide you," you might end up on the beach rather than the dock.

We'll talk more about how people can influence us and how to overcome that influence. For now, keep the potential for influence in mind as you complete the 20 Goals Exercise.

Now that you have a better understanding of your definition of success, you can set your goals. Once you have an idea of what your goals are, your journey begins. Part one of this book describes the goal-setting process.

Second Mouse Concept Four: Setting your Course

Being your own worst enemy sabotages your success, so your next step is navigating the mediocrity trap. Don't let your doubts overwhelm you; you can get stuck in the mediocrity trap when you wallow in your self-doubt, enabling your negative thoughts and self-talk to drive your actions and take over: "I'm too old, or I'm too fat, or I'm too this, or I'm too that."

Pop culture reinforces the mediocrity trap, as do the people around us. Surprisingly, the people who care about you can be the most destructive. They love you, and they don't want you to get hurt, so they caution you, unintentionally discouraging you from achieving your goals. As discussed earlier, they also have their ideas of success that can distract you and steer you away from your goals.

We have all gone through this in one way or another. I give real-life examples to help navigate the mediocrity trap.

Second Mouse Concept Five: Your Tools

The good news is that when you understand your definition of success and know what you want, you have the tools you need to achieve your goals.

You have:

1. Your Mind
2. Your Body
3. Your Brand
4. Your Team

The first two are probably familiar to you, and the last two might be new.

Mind

No matter the age or stage in your life, you need to feed your mind. It is crucial as you get older. One of the age stereotypes is that older people are behind the times. If you are going to overcome stereotypes and remain relevant, you need to feed your mind continually.

Reading – Written material is the most convenient source of information. You need to read! It doesn't matter what you read, as both fiction and nonfiction can give you examples of life experiences.

Classes – Taking classes is essential in learning and staying relevant. There are free classes everywhere, on the internet, in schools, and in less formal settings. There are also paid classes, like college courses, continuing education courses, and seminars. Since you are reading this, you already see the value of learning new things. Now, you need to do it as much as you can.

Coaches –One of my favorite learning sources is coaches, and I have a few. They are experts who can guide me through specific areas and help me with different parts of my life.

- An executive coach helps me with my career.
- A fitness coach helps me get into better shape.
- A sensei helps me grow in my martial arts.

These people can each give you specific feedback on a particular area of your life. Information from coaches is personal and relevant; you can't get it from a book or a class. Their input is invaluable and can give you a head start on life changes.

Body

You have one body for life; you can't trade it in for a newer model, so you need to take care of it. Another age stereotype to consider as you get older is that older people lack energy. It is hard to say you are a high-energy individual if you get winded walking up the stairs.

Having energy does not mean that you need to be an Olympic athlete to succeed. I am not slim, but I am working on getting slimmer. Taking care of your body in this context is all about diet and exercise. You can succeed if you are out of shape, but a lack of fitness makes it that much more challenging. Poor choices in this area can sabotage your achievement. If I were nervous about a presentation and overindulged in comfort food and a few drinks beforehand, I would not be at my best. It would help if you were mindful of your level of fitness and diet.

Brand

Your brand; this concept in this context may be new to you. When we talk about brands, most tend to think about a company or a product. When you buy paper towels, you want durable paper towels that cost less, not a soggy nor expensive paper towel. You want your brand to reflect who you really are, and you most certainly don't want people to see you as a soggy paper towel. Your brand must show the value you offer to others. My local bank strives to be people-oriented. They want to help the community as well as individuals, whether they are customers or not. I like that, and that is why I choose to bank with them. If I call the vice president, she will remember me and help me with an account or even non-banking requests. Their sincere sense of community is evident. It is their brand.

You need to think about other people's perceptions when you are developing your personal brand. Let me tell you a story of an incident just a week before I wrote this paragraph. I worked for a company with two giant snack drawers (one for salty snacks and one for sweet snacks). After a particularly stressful day, everyone knew that I would partake in the drawers' contents. On this particular day, we had a consultant helping us with some process improvements. He saw me at the snack drawer and asked, "Are you sure you want to grab a snack?" After reading some of my online content, he believed grabbing a snack did not fit my brand because of my focus on personal fitness and healthy living.

Confronting me directly on my snack choices might have been rude, but it highlighted how people perceive me but may not bring to my attention when I don't live up to my brand. When it comes to my book, part of my brand is paying attention to my diet, and having Oreo cookies does not support that brand.

If I do not live my brand, my credibility will be in jeopardy. You need to live your brand.

Team

The last tool is your team. The team can be the most challenging tool to employ because you must consciously choose your team members. The people who care about you most (family, close friends) can be some of the worst teammates. Sadly, they can be biased and may actually discourage you from your goals because they want to protect you from failure and are afraid you will get hurt.

Also, like any other team, you need specific players.

The ideal team will have:

Sponsors – These are the people who pull you up. They can be bosses or other leaders that encourage you and want to help you grow.

Coaches/Mentors – I differential between coaches and mentors by whether you pay them. By my definition, you pay coaches, not mentors. We talked about coaches earlier. Mentors are people with whom you have a personal relationship that give you advice. I have several mentors. You probably have many, but you may not think of them in such a formal way.

Peers – These are the people you surround yourself with, your coworkers, friends, etc. Remember that it is hard to soar with the eagles when you surround yourself with turkeys.

Subordinates – These are not just people who work for you. These are people you are helping in their growth; you are their sponsor or mentor, and in return, they do things for you. I often use my kids as an example. They complete tasks that free me up to do more important tasks, and in return, I give them guidance and support.

Notice that I called this your team rather than your service providers. Except for the coach, these are not people you pay. You need to build relationships with these people and have a sincere attitude of giving, as they have no compulsion to help you. You may give much more than you receive, but you will find that people will be more willing to help you as you help others.

You have these tools at your disposal. Some factors that you have no control over can affect the first two. The good news is that you can compensate for any weaknesses found in the first two by emphasizing the second two.

A vital principle of this book is the idiom that all ships rise with the tide. The team is an integral part of success, and we need to help each other grow; by serving others to grow ourselves.

> *"You can have everything in life you want, if you will just help other people get what they want."*
>
> — ZIG ZIGLAR

Using the Second Mouse Philosophy

How you define success is personal. What success means can be a tricky question to answer, and only you can determine what success means to you. You may have considered your goals and think that you have an idea of what success means. You can probably categorize your goals:

- Goals at work
- Family goals

- Things you wish to acquire

We will explore whether these goals fit your definition of success.

A major takeaway from this book is that you need to act if you want results. That may sound very basic but look back at your New Years' resolutions. Are you still working on those resolutions? What are your results? We will address several ideas, like setting and achieving personal goals; and networking to build your team and identify potential mentors.

Specifically, this book covers how you can change plans into action and how you can build your teams to be successful.

In the end, we fail because we do not take ownership of the goal and give up on the continuous and consistent action needed. The Second Mouse Philosophy provides a framework to set you on the course for success.

What's next?

I have divided the book into sections.

- Part One – Your Goals
- Part Two – Taking Action
- Part Three – Building Relationships/Networking
- Part Four – Building Mentor Relationships
- Executing The Plan – Avoid the Trap and Get the Cheese

Each chapter ends with a Reflection, a Takeaway, a Results, and a Notes section. The notes section gives you a place to record your thoughts. In addition, I recommend that you use a notebook as a journal. When you get to the Reflection and Takeaway sections, write down the answers to the questions and anything that struck you. The results section will give you examples of how using the techniques in the chapter can positively affect your life.

This book can guide you in building the life you were meant to live. You just need to put in the work.

Right now, you have the tools you need to succeed! Let's get to work!

PART 1
YOUR GOALS

CHAPTER 1
Your Goals Need To Be Your Own

You emulate the people around you, and those people influence your actions, behavior, and aspirations. The people around you can affect you so much that you can recognize the goals they project as your goals.

> *"You're the average of the five people you spend most of your time with."*
>
> — JIM ROHN

Working on goals that are not your own can negatively impact your life in several ways.

1. It can affect your self-esteem. You work hard but feel like you are in a hamster wheel getting nowhere and unworthy of success. I was looking at a picture of a shipwreck. A giant cargo ship stuck on a beach; everything of value was stripped away, and it was stained from stem to stern in graffiti. I saw myself in that picture. There have been times in my life when I've been stuck; it is when I was stuck that my confidence was

stripped away, and others' opinions stained my ideas. How do you feel when you are stuck?

2. Compensating can negatively impact your health. We tend to compensate for holes in our lives with offsetting behaviors. If you are stressed or depressed, you might use food, alcohol, or excessive television watching to compensate for what you miss. I feed my problems and gain weight because I feel like I'm not achieving my goals when I get stressed out and use food as my coping mechanism. These destructive behaviors can impact your health.

3. You can also experience relationship issues. When you experience difficulties in your life, you can project these into other areas, like your relationships. This projection can lead you to believe that the issues you are having at work are actually marital issues. Have you ever had a bad day at work and come home only to take it out on your family for no reason?

When you don't follow your dreams, you will probably use destructive behavior to compensate for that bad feeling. Throughout my life, I have had trouble identifying my goals. I would get wrapped up in volunteer activities at the expense of work, take classes and never act on them, get to the five-yard line and be called back by the siren's call of safety, or merely get wrapped up in other people's ambitions. I would see others succeed and feel stuck; I have used destructive behaviors to compensate for not following my dreams. Destructive behaviors are great at distracting you from the real problem. You can go through your whole life chasing the wrong issues, distracting yourself enough, so you never pursue your goals and never reach the level of success you could have.

I have always felt the influences of other people's goals. I felt like I was not achieving my full potential but stayed the course because it was the "right thing to do." It felt safe. These influencers can change your mind in such a subtle way that you feel like it was your decision. I believed that the thing my influencers wanted me to do was the "right thing to do." I allowed them to project their fear onto me and amplify my insecurities, believing that achieving their goals for them was actually my goal. However, these projected goals put me on the wrong path. Seeing people happy in their jobs would make me wonder what I was doing wrong. I had mentors and coaches telling me to change my focus. Instead of listening, I would stay in my comfort zone, following my influencers' path of least resistance.

In my comfort zone, I was busy all the time. I filled my days with distractions and my influencers' feedback because my focus was on their goals rather than my own. I worked for a company whose owner had a cult leader-like personality. I was part of the management team who would strive for his approval, like children with an absent parent. In return, we would get distrust and micromanagement and would respond with the thought: "well, if I only did a little more, he would trust me, and I can succeed." We were busy for the sake of being busy, knowing that we were wasting time and were not as effective as we could have been, but we continued because "it was the right thing to do."

I believe in taking responsibility for the results I produce, but being results rather than task-oriented hurt me in this environment because the company focussed on activity rather than results, a culture that discouraged efficient work in favor of being excessively busy. This environment's toxicity was hard to recognize because the person we worked for was generally inspiring and a good person.

The owner's inability to make timely decisions and his extreme fear of missing out exacerbated the issue. It caused a level of micromanagement that negated any opportunities for employees' personal growth. It had all of the attributes of a company that offered career growth and a workplace that could almost be successful, except the leadership was unwilling to let the team shine.

Until I recognized the trap, I had altered my goals and tried to succeed in an environment that only gave the appearance of opportunity. Even after acknowledging that I was not working toward my goals, it wasn't easy because the people around me were still futilely trying to succeed in that environment. At some level, the others also recognized the problem. One of my peers constantly asked me if I was looking for a new job before going through reasons people should leave. Another peer would lament that it was too late for him to make any changes when we talked about work. These comments and thoughts from peers were unsolicited.

It is essential to get out of the weeds, take a step back and consider an unbiased opinion of your situation. I needed a lifeline to get out of my funk. My executive coach helped me recognize how toxic my situation was. Look carefully at your situation and, if needed, get an independent view. With that impartial opinion, you need to determine how others influence you and if their influence is hurting you. Do others influence you to achieve their goals? Are you ignoring your goals to help them achieve theirs?

Once you've determined what you want, you need to seek advice. Where is the best place to start? It would be best if you asked experts. People who know what they're talking about, who have done what you want to do, who could show you the way, who can give you shortcuts, who could teach and encourage you, as well as discourage you from making mistakes. However, we typically resort to asking the people around us instead. It is easier to reach out to those around you than to seek out the experts.

Potentially, getting advice from the inexperienced people around you makes you the first mouse, and the trap is waiting to snap. Seeking advice and guidance from experts, who have been the first mouse, sets you well on the second mouse's path circumventing the trap.

Sadly, these people around us are influencers. These are the people in your life who push you this way and push you that way, just like tugboats push ships. They push you in various directions that may or may not drive you towards your goal.

Now, who are these influencers?

Family: The people who love you most want to protect you from failure and don't want you to get hurt. They don't want you to take risks, so they will push you to avoid any risks. Their actions are comforting but not helpful, especially if they have no expertise in the areas you are considering. Also, their influence is not always innocent; many family members want you to participate in activities so that they can live vicariously through you.

Friends: your friends want to support you, but they might want to avoid change and influence your desire for change. When I was younger, I was a lot heavier and liked the idea of participating in a triathlon. I knew that I was too heavy, but maybe I could achieve this goal if I worked out. So, chatting to my friends in a bar, I told them of my plan, and they said, "Chad, you know that triathlons aren't smoking, drinking, and eating, right? With that comment, my desire to pursue completing a triathlon died.

Workmates: your coworkers and bosses can direct you with rewards and punishments, pushing you in different directions that may or may not fit your intentions. I worked for a company that loaned money to people with terrible credit. The use of rewards and threats directed my work. It was a toxic environment, but I wanted to be successful, so I would strive to earn the rewards, and I was successful, but I didn't feel successful because achieving those rewards wasn't bringing me closer to my goals. I was reaching the company's objectives, which conflicted with mine. There were also threats.

I remember a particular meeting close to Christmas; it was festive, with decorations, and they served cake. The company fostered a high-pressure, high-stress sales environment, and we had had a stressful but profitable year. We were in the meeting talking to one another and decompressing when the VP of sales stood up. We were looking forward to that year-end motivational speech expressing appreciation for our hard work this year. He started by asking a question: "what holiday is coming at the end of this month?" We all looked at each other, and someone sheepishly said, "Well, that's, ah, Christmas." The VP says, "That's right, and how long has Christmas been around again?" This time, a little less sheepishly, someone said, "Well, it's been around for 2000 years." The VP replied, "Good. So we all know that Christmas is coming and we've known for 2000 years. **I do not want to hear one of you say** you missed your target because of Christmas!" Work influences like these can damage your self-esteem, making you feel like you are working hard with no reward. You start seeing that achieving other people's goals at the expense of your own can have personal consequences.

Reflection

Review your goals. Why do you want to achieve those goals?

Do those reasons correspond to your definition of success?

Complete the 20 goals exercise to see how your goals relate to your definition of success.

Think about who the influencers are in your life are;

- your family,
- your friends,
- your coworkers.

Who influences you? Is it positive or negative? Write down how they influence you and how that impacts your life. What lessons can you learn from that influence? This exercise will help you determine whose goals you're following. Are you following your goals, or are you following someone else's? It's important to determine whose goals you're following because if you're not pursuing your own goals, there will always be that nagging lack of achievement ache.

Are you using compensating behaviors or projecting your frustration at not following your goals in other areas of your life?

It is essential to reflect on how satisfied you are with your life. Look back and think about your regrets. What do you feel you should have done? What paths should you have followed? What is holding you back? What do you need to do to move forward? Write down your thoughts. Your ideas won't come all at once, so journaling will help you gather your ideas over time.

I want you to imagine yourself five years from now, in a place where you have achieved your desired goals. What does your life look like now? You may want to put the book down and get a pen and paper. Be specific in your thoughts. What have you accomplished, and how did you achieve it?

Now, come back to this moment. What action can you take today to start you on the path leading to that place five years in the future? Are you willing to take that step today, right now? If you aren't ready, what actions do you need to take to focus on your goals? Write down your obstacles, and let's look at them.

Takeaway

There can be consequences to not pursuing your goals.

- Self Esteem
- Health Issues
- Relationship Issues

Setting clear goals requires an understanding of your definition of success

Your definition of success is personal, so only you can determine what success means to you.

Your success is your responsibility.

Results

You can feel it when you aren't genuinely following your goals. I find the feeling to be reminiscent of the end of the school year. Remember your school days; it is mid-June, there were many snow days, so you are still in school beyond the scheduled end of the school year. No one wants to be in school anymore, not you, not the other kids, not even the teachers.

The feeling that you want to be doing something else is so palpable; you can almost feel it physically. The summer is calling you, and you feel trapped in the classroom. That is how it feels when you are ignoring your goals to focus on other people's goals.

Focusing on our goals helps us defeat our enemy, complacency. Complacency causes you to miss opportunities. By focusing on your goals, you can build your confidence and live the life you want to live.

NOTES

NOTES

NOTES

CHAPTER 2
Beyond Planning - Avoiding The Mediocrity Trap

It's time to turn the lens on yourself. You have to be honest and thorough when looking at yourself. The only effective way to plan to get where you want to go is to have a complete understanding of where you are now. If you are trying to lose weight, you won't know how much weight you have to lose unless you weigh yourself; it gives you a baseline to measure your progress. The Second Mouse Philosophy uses the OODA Loop to determine where you are, what you need to do to reach your objective, and how to get beyond planning.

The OODA loop, developed by John Boyd, a United States Air Force Colonel and military strategist, is a process to assess a situation and act. He developed this concept to improve the combat operations process during military campaigns. The OODA (Observe, Orient, Decide, Act) Loop is a process for tactics to instill the propensity for action.

I am using the example of losing weight. You understand the strategy of burning more calories than you consume; now, what are you going to do?

1. Observe – You weigh yourself and determine that you need to lose 20 pounds.
2. Orient – You realize that you can improve your diet and start exercising.
3. Decide – You put together a plan to lose 20 pounds.
4. Act – You execute the diet and exercise plan.

The example includes one goal for simplicity, but we will be using the OODA Loop to achieve your broader life goals.

Observe

Since you are building a plan for yourself, you need to understand where you are now; you get this information by performing a self-analysis. In addition to goal-related details, what else should you consider when completing this self-analysis?

1. **Your fears** – what are you afraid of, and how will that affect your progress?
2. **Are you too closed** – are you unable to be vulnerable? Are you closed to opportunities?
3. **Do you have clarity** – you need a clear picture of where you want to go. It is hard to get there if you don't know where you are going.
4. **Priorities** – are you spreading yourself too thin with too many initiatives. Remember that if everything is a priority, nothing is.

5. **Focus** – are you able to focus on a goal. If not, challenging goals may be out of your reach.

Orient

Now that you have determined where you are on your journey, what do you need to achieve your goals? Just like school, you need to complete your prerequisites.

- You need to complete the first grade to move to the second grade.
- You need to complete primary school to move to middle school.
- Each year of education prepares you for the next year of your learning and life.

You need to connect your current situation to your goal achievement by orienting yourself and identifying all of the prerequisites to complete this journey. Documenting these steps is your plan, and completing them is your preparation. If you are running a race, you need to practice running and start perfecting your form. If you are testing for a martial arts belt, you need to practice your forms and sparring. Why wouldn't you prepare for your life goals? Don't take these for granted.

We tend to focus on local targets. By that, I mean we focus on single-purpose goals. We want to lose weight to get healthy or to look good. We go to softball practice to get better at softball. Where do you go to be better at living? Where do you go to connect the dots? How do you open yourself up to see why you are not reaching the objectives you set for yourself?

Since we have never looked at what success means to us, we've never focused on an overall goal plan. I read a book on manufacturing theory called "The Goal" by Eliyahu M. Goldratt. One of the things he addresses in the book is focusing on local optima. Manufacturing companies would talk about how they improved efficiencies in a specific department, but the company's overall output has not changed. So improving efficiency in one area had no impact on the process's overall efficiency, and the plant was not better off.

The same principle applies to people. We focus on local optima and address minor personal improvements in isolation from your overall goals. How do your local successes help you achieve your overall goals? Do they help you, or are they hindering you? If you work in a toxic work environment that negatively affects your health, family life, and other aspects of your life and get a promotion, do you celebrate? Is that promotion a win, or is it a distraction from your real goals? Is the distraction reeling you away from your goals like a fish on a line?

In the example above, the promotion, while an achievement, can move you farther away from the goals that lead to your definition of success. The potential for misdirection is why you must have a clear understanding of what success means to you. Without it, you can go through life accepting these isolated wins but constantly feeling inside that you are actually losing. You have this little internal voice that knows you are not on the path to achieving your goals. Still, your focus is scattered on multiple isolated wins because you have not established your comprehensive life goals.

If you are still unclear on what your goals are, refer back to chapter 1. If you have an idea of what your goals are, let's move forward and get beyond planning. Take this part seriously. Yes, you know yourself better than anyone else, but that does not mean you know yourself well. Open your mind and see what areas need to improve to achieve your goals. Make sure you took enough time to get to the truth in Chapter 1, otherwise you risk wasting time on the wrong path.

Decide

I do not want to discount the importance of planning. I spend a lot of time planning both my personal and work goals. As described in the orient section above, you must take the time to plan. However, the point comes when planning needs to stop, and you need to make a decision. Planning is an integral part of achieving goals, but it is also a trap. You can get so wrapped up in planning that you never execute your plans. You can get stuck in a couple of areas:

1. The fear of missing something
2. Lack of execution

By making a decision, you put a stake in the ground that you are ready to achieve your goals. No decision is perfect, and there is always the risk that you will miss something because you will never have all of the information. Even with the risk associated with doing new things, you will feel better about yourself and your situation once you make your decision.

Taking the first step is the hardest. It is much easier to continue to plan and analyze. If you follow the path of least resistance, you will never execute the plan; this resistance to execution makes the decision so important. By making a decision, you reset the starting line and close the planning stage. You are ready to take action.

Act

You made a decision, and now the work needs to begin. Ideas do not bring results. Actions bring results. You will never achieve your goals by sitting in a conference room talking about plans or sitting on your couch daydreaming. You need to take action!

Remember that you have just written your plans on paper, not carved them in stone. As you are working, you can review your progress and determine how your plans are working toward achieving your goals. If they are not working, YOU CAN CHANGE THEM! If you **observe** that things have changed, there is no reason you can't **orient** through updated planning, **decide** to make some changes, and **act** on those changes. (sound familiar?)

Taking action is critical if you want to achieve goals, but action can make you feel uncomfortable, especially if you are doing something new or challenging. Sitting with friends talking about doing things is comfortable; we all find comfort in the warmth of potential. You think about all the great things you can do, and you feel good. Going into the cold, unpredictable world of action can be scary and stressful, but you need to enter this world if you want to succeed. Action leads to results!

Cheese Box

Taking Action with a Goal Focus

Goal Focus – Be a Participant, not a spectator!

I worked with someone who was addicted to the show Shark Tank. He watched it religiously and would talk about it at work. Instead of being inspired by the shows' participants, he lived vicariously through them. He would spend his time being a spectator with no accomplishments of his own to reflect on.

Shows like Shark Tank can be entertaining, and there is nothing wrong with watching them. What is more concerning is how you react to them. Are you inspired, or are you projecting others' success on yourself so you can revel in it without achieving your own?

If you revel in the success of others, you stifle your growth. It is often evident in children's sports with parents living through their children, rather than striving themselves.

Goal Focus -Preparation

Athletes prepare for the big game. Astronauts prepare before they go into space. You need to prepare for your goals. The importance of preparation is especially evident when you are working on big goals. There are things you can do to prepare in parallel to your striving to achieve your goals.

To achieve goals, especially big goals, you need to take them seriously and be willing to prepare yourself to achieve them.

Preparation includes:

- Developing Yourself
- Learning Required Skills
- Be Open to New Ideas
- Focus on Your Goals
- Build Confidence Over Time
- Eliminate Destructive Behaviors
- Environment
- Understand How Influencers Affect You

Goal Focus – Avoid shiny things

When fishing, people use different types of bait. A kind of fishing lure reflects light, and in the water, it is shiny to get the fish's attention and encourages the fish to chase it. Those "interesting ideas" do the same thing to you. You are swimming along trying to reach your goals, and a shiny thing is put in front of you, and you chase it. Before you catch it, you see another shiny thing and chase that one and so on and so on.

Eventually you lose track of your goal because you were chasing shiny things. You need to have discipline to achieve your goals. You need to want to achieve your goal so much you can taste it. You have to keep your eyes on the prize and avoid shiny things, which is easier said than done. You need to develop the discipline to avoid distractions.

"When you want to succeed as bad as you want to breathe, then you'll be successful."
— ERIC THOMAS

While socializing your idea or just thinking about it yourself, it can be easy to get sidetracked and distracted from the real goal. Gathering information can cause information overload and encourage you to chase shiny things. When writing my book and socializing it, I got a lot of feedback, some big ideas, and some great ones that had nothing to do with the topic I was developing. They were interesting ideas, but they were distractions.

Goal Focus - Stay on target

I have a poster in my office of the targeting system from the X-wing fighter attacking the Death Star in Star Wars, A New Hope with the caption "Stay on Target" The goal of a group of fighters destroying the Death Star is a big goal. There were significant obstacles, the distraction of enemy fighters shooting at them, and severe consequences for failure. Keeping focused was imperative since defeat would have been devastating to their cause.

Take responsibility for your workspace. Set it up to eliminate as many distractions as possible. Understand your goals and set yourself up for success.

This strategy ia vital as you need to prepare yourself and your environment to remain focused. If you are giving up your job to start a business, chasing shiny things can cost you your income.

If you are working on a side-gig, shiny things can derail your success. People give up on themselves, thinking they can't achieve their goals when they are just overwhelmed by distractions.

You want the same focus on your goals. When those distractions start to attract your attention, "Stay on target!"

Goal Focus – Prioritize

How important are your goals to you? Are you willing to sacrifice for them? Your focus will determine how effective you will be in achieving your goals. You can have multiple and diverse goals. I want to succeed in my job, I want to write books, I want to be a keynote speaker, and I want to live a healthy life. Work on each goal without being distracted by the others. When working at my job, I need to focus on that, not my book. That does not mean that I complete my goals in isolation. Should an idea for my writing pop up while at work, I'll write it down for later and get back to work.

Record your thoughts when you find inspiration, but don't try to multi-task. Be engaged in your work so you can achieve your work-related goals. At work, we joke that we are saving the world one loan at a time, but the work we do is essential, and mistakes can cost the company hundreds of thousands of dollars. We need to navigate the obstacles and stay on target. I use notebooks and journals to capture ideas to record my thoughts, and they are not lost. Then I can get back to the task at hand.

You can do the same thing. Have notebooks in the areas you work and think (I even have them in my car).

Unless you decide to take an active role in determining your success, the factors we described in this chapter lead us to give up on your goals. Over time, you will give away your power, time, and dreams for relatively small rewards.

Instead of focusing on goals, we tend to listen to our influencers and follow the path of least resistance, which pushes us away from our goals to focus on low hanging fruit:

- Salary

- Security
- Leisure
- Distractions

Using the reflection exercises, get a firm understanding of your goals and how people influence you. Also, understand how you use destructive behaviors to compensate for not following your goals.

I am emphasizing these points for a reason. Take a moment to think about your goals. How many times have you pushed the start of a fitness plan to "next Monday"? We have all dwelt in planning and avoided action with statements like "I will achieve "FILL IN THE BLANK" after "SOME ARTIFICIAL DEADLINE.""

Once you have taken action, you will have a sense of satisfaction from driving your future even before seeing results. Take action, achieve your goals, and avoid the mediocrity trap!

You want to succeed and inherently know that you have to take action to achieve those goals, but you also have insecurities and fears. Your planning is complete, and you will start tomorrow, start Monday, or start at the beginning of the year. Postponing your start with reasons that seem to make sense to you are distractions in actuality.

Here are three types of distractions that can prevent or delay your start:

1. Procrastination strategies.
2. Instant entertainment.
3. Artificial success programs.

We have all used procrastination strategies to prevent us from doing a difficult, tedious, or scary task. We need to do X before we do Y. And even though X is not a prerequisite of Y, we convince ourselves that the distraction is actually part of the plan.

Instant entertainment is a relatively new phenomenon, although younger readers have had it for most of their lives. There are posts, videos, and cat pictures offering instant entertainment anytime, anywhere. I read an article that smoking and drinking among the younger generation has declined because they can address boredom and discomfort with this alternative entertainment method.

Instant entertainment is an easy distraction that can keep you from achieving your goals. I will often take a quick break from my work and watch old comedy videos; before I know it, Rodney Dangerfield and Richard Pryor have stolen two hours, and I have not accomplished my goals.

> **"The people will not revolt. They will not look up from their screens long enough to notice what's happening"**
> — GEORGE ORWELL, 1984

Although we are not worried about being brainwashed by the government, we must be concerned about the valuable time wasted on instant entertainment rather than using it wisely to achieve our goals.

I call the last distraction an artificial success program and have identified two types.

1. Online empire building.

2. Volunteer leadership as a replacement for career success.

Online empire-building games are perpetual, and success takes a material amount of time. When I was younger, I played "Mafia Wars" on Facebook. Instead of watching television, I would play; but soon found that I would be "attacked" when I was offline. I became obsessed with it, causing me to start checking it during the day, which led me to start playing during the day rather than working. I stopped playing because it was now interfering with my performance.

Many empire-building games are available; they are fun and give you a sense of achieving goals, but these are artificial. They give you instant gratification but then leave you empty as it is hard to have any lasting pride in achieving a new level in a game.

The other distraction is volunteer leadership as a replacement for career success. Volunteering and taking leadership positions in volunteer organizations are critical tasks. You should volunteer more and take leadership positions giving you an even more significant positive impact on your communities and those in need. However, you must be careful of the leadership trap of volunteer organizations. Volunteering can give you an incredible feeling of success that you dedicate more time to volunteering and use it as a replacement for achieving personal goals. I urge you to volunteer and help people but do not let that satisfaction distract you from your plans.

"We never failed to fail; it was the easiest thing to do."
— CROSBY, STILLS, NASH AND YOUNG

Besides distractions, some tend to belittle themselves to the point of feeling that they don't have the skills, energy, or time to succeed. Coming up with reasons to fail causes many to not even try. That must be flipped around and say what needs to be done to achieve the goals. What must I learn? What actions must I take? Then take those actions.

Don't sell yourself short. You have the skills to achieve your goals or at least transferable skills that you can sharpen with a bit of coaching. Even if you have no particular knowledge to accomplish something, the resources are available to get that knowledge. There are numerous free and paid courses and resources on the web and classes to take; all just a short online search away.

A little more hands-on knowledge or one-on-one instruction from a coach or mentor might be the way to go; this will be covered in more detail later in the book. You may consider some volunteer work in the area you want to explore. My son is considering a career in law enforcement. A friend told me about the local police citizen's course, which seemed like an excellent resource for determining whether or not you would like to be a police officer. My son applied and starts soon. He can then make an informed decision if it is the right choice for him.

Again, the key is to act. It is easier to fret about not having skills than going out to get them. If you want to be good at something, you have to have the courage to be bad at it until you get good at it!

Everyone has fear. What do you do when you are afraid? We may hide under the metaphorical bed, or we may build the metaphorical fort. With our defenses up, we close the doors and peek through the windows. If fictional bad guys are chasing us, this might be the correct response; however, it becomes a problem when the fear reaction rears its head when trying to achieve your goals.

- Driving to a job interview – the little voice in your head tells you, you aren't worthy. You start to sweat and get the urge to go home.
- Thinking about starting a business – The negative statistics and friends comments that you should keep your good job, as a good job is hard to find.
- You want to buy a house – What if you lose your job, what if the furnace breaks. You could lose everything.

When planning, you are working with limited information. You cannot predict the future, so you need to make assumptions. These assumptions are best if you base them on experience and a broad knowledge base, but they are still assumptions. You need to plan with the best information you have and not get trapped in a discussion whirlpool, talking yourself in circles and never reaching a conclusion. You have to accept that you will never have all of the information you need, and there is always risk in action. You want to limit that risk, but you must understand that you can never eliminate it.

If you are cautious, weigh risks, and avoid pitfalls. Are you prudent, or are you fearful?

We tend to be over-cautious. Everyone has a fear of failure, and we have an amazing ability to see the worst possibilities in any situation. We can choose to hide behind the veil of caution because we are actually afraid to try. Action is a cure for fear!

Getting over fear is selling yourself on the concept that you can accomplish your goals. You can do this by:

- Being vulnerable
- Surrounding yourself with supportive people
- Learning more about the task you want to complete

What if, what if, what if.... How do you react to difficult situations? Do you close in and dwell in your thoughts or open up to the potential of failure or rejection? If you are going to reach your full potential, you need to open up. You need to be vulnerable, which can be difficult.

We are taught to be strong and independent to do things on our own. We are not encouraged to put ourselves in situations that might lead to failure or criticism. We are fed the illusion that success is a straight line. We believe that failing is the opposite of success rather than part of the process to reach success. All of this pushes you to avoid being vulnerable. When studying martial arts, I learned a couple of vulnerability lessons. I studied non-traditional styles that allowed me to rely on my size and strength, but as I got older, I realized that I needed to think about protecting myself using technique rather than strength.

After achieving black belt level in two styles, a very traditional teacher invited me to train in a new discipline. I thought I would pick up the techniques immediately and be on my way to another black belt. I was mistaken. There was so much that I didn't understand. In class, my ego told me to leave and go back to what I know, and the little voice told me that you can't teach old dogs new tricks. It took time; it took being humble and open to criticism. I put myself in the vulnerable position of being a novice again. I needed to be willing to do something poorly to get to the point that I could do it well.

It would help if you considered this when getting yourself ready to achieve your goals. You need to:

1. Determine if you already have the skills or if you need training.
2. Determine the skills you need help with.
3. Identify a source for obtaining those skills.
4. Put effort into learning new or improving existing skills.
5. Be willing to do something poorly to reach the point to do it well
6. Be open to criticism.

I needed to be vulnerable with the courage to perform poorly until I learned to perform well; it came with criticism and corrections. It is not easy!

Another personal example is when I asked people for feedback before publishing my first book. I wanted criticism when I asked for it but found that I did not like it when I received it. I had to continually remind myself that I asked for the criticism, needed the criticism, and had to accept that it was constructive and not a personal attack. Getting constructive criticism is an integral part of learning but can be hard to take; you need to be vulnerable and open to criticism for this. It is a skill that does not come easily, especially when the critique is on something you have worked on for a year.

Cheese Box

Elements of Constructive Criticism

1. Trust – the person needs to have your best interests at heart.
2. Knowledge/Experience – The person needs to have the knowledge and experience required to offer constructive feedback.
3. Rapport – You need to be able to relate to the person.

Be willing to do something poorly until you can do it well. Find the sources of knowledge you require and put the time in to learn. Be vulnerable, and open yourself up to criticism.

Understand that criticism and failure are part of your success journey. Expect criticism and for your friends and family to question your judgment. By carefully selecting the people you need to support you, you can filter out the noise and use the relevant criticism to direct you toward your goals. We are searching for people with experience and the willingness to tell us the hard truths so we can improve. We want to filter out the people who just compliment our work, people with uninformed opinions, and those who are disrespectful don't have your best interests at heart.

The people around you have a considerable impact on you; if they feed your fear, your fear will grow. There will always be people who will feed your fears. You can insulate yourself by choosing a support circle that will help you overcome those fears. Building your support circle is no easy task; it takes a lot of research and relationship building. You are interviewing people like you would hire someone, just in a less formal process, but the goal is the same. You want to find people who give you the support you need.

I have developed a circle with a variety of people that I meet to discuss ideas. One person I meet a couple of times a month, but others I only talk to perhaps once a year. These people do not pat me on the back and say, "good job Chad." They are all busy people who don't have time to dawdle. I contact them with purpose, and they respond with purpose.

When you build your circle, you need to consider your needs carefully. Do you need:

- Emotional Support
- Career Guidance
- Information on New Endeavors
- Skill Training

Adding people who have achieved what you want to accomplish to your circle also helps. Talking to someone who has done what you are looking to achieve can give you insights you can't get from a book. There are retired people and people outside your market area to add to your circle that you can go to for advice. Having that lifeline will help you work through many moments of anxiety.

Ignorance feeds fear. If you do not know how something is going to turn out, you get nervous. Suppose you have to give a speech to a room of strangers and don't know how they will react. You are nervous. Boxers watch their opponent's previous fights; they study their style and understand what to expect when they fight.

Getting information that shows you can succeed will help you get over your fear. Getting information is different from getting support. When you need information, you don't need someone to tell you that you can do anything you set your mind to. You need someone who has done what you want to do or knows how to do it to give you the information you need to be successful.

That information will give you the knowledge you need to move forward, and your fear will wane.

A great example of something we can all use help on is public speaking. Whether you have never done it before or are an accomplished speaker, there is always room to improve. The best program to learn public speaking at any level that I have found is Toastmasters. Toastmasters is an international organization with the mission to teach its members public speaking and leadership skills.

Standing in front of a crowd to speak, whether it is ten people or 1000 people, you make yourself vulnerable. You are opening yourself up to the potential of criticism (not the constructive type). That exposure causes anxiety, so much so that people avoid public speaking even if it can help them achieve their goals.

Toastmasters offers a nurturing environment that allows the member to proceed at their own pace. They give the tools needed to create and deliver a speech and people to coach and mentor them along the way. Finally, they offer a friendly environment to the new speaker to perform their speech and get feedback that teaches them how to improve without ruining their confidence. They get to perform poorly in a friendly environment until they perform well. They are well prepared and present in an outside environment with the confidence to do well right out of the gate.

The Toastmasters model is a good one to follow for any skills you need to learn. Get expert help, find a comfortable and friendly environment to perfect your skills, and go out and use them.

Reflection

It is time to determine where you are in your path. In chapter one, you identified your goals. Now you need to determine what to do to achieve them. Using the OODA Loop, develop and execute your plan. Using your journal, capture observations about yourself, your environment, your challenges, and your advantages. Now orient yourself. Using your observations, decide on the direction you need to take to achieve your goals? What preparation do you require? This analysis has probably provided you with several options. Review these and decide which one you want to follow. Now it is time to act.

Just as you did with your goal setting, take your time; it is okay if you spend a couple of weeks or a month on this. Just don't get stuck in the mediocrity trap of never executing. Remember that these plans are written on paper, not carved in stone, so you can make adjustments as you move along. As you are recording and detailing your goals in your plan, look for patterns. These patterns will help you consolidate your goals into comprehensive life goals.

We will be using the OODA Loop throughout the book. Please review it and make sure you understand it.

Takeaways

First, you need to plan with your path written on paper. You need to set a timeframe, with a clear endpoint, to put your plan together.

Second, you need to take action. That action may not be to execute your plan; it may be the preparation. If your objective is to get a new job, it is not always wise to quit your job before having an alternative. As preparation, you want to network with people to see what else is out there and interview for other jobs while working. If you are starting a business, you may want to do this part-time to maintain your lifestyle while moving toward your goal. Being a starving artist sounds romantic, but having your electricity turned off is no fun.

Three, you don't know everything. Be open to learning. Allow yourself to be vulnerable and understand it is okay to be bad at something until you can do it well. When you have been successful, it is hard to start something where you are not proficient.

The key is to plan and then move forward with intention. You need to be thoughtful but have a propensity for action. Think about Isaac Newton's laboratory. An object in motion stays in motion, and an object at rest stays at rest. You want to be the object in motion, but you don't want to be bouncing all over the place like a super ball; you want to have a plan that directs your action in line with your goals.

> *"For when men labor, they keep out of mischief. You remember the old proverb--An idle mind is the Devil's workshop."*
>
> — GEORGE Q. CANNON

Action is a cure to fear. Doing something keeps the mind busy, and there is no time to worry about the worst-case scenario. When you add purpose (your goals), you conquer your fear and get the satisfaction of working toward your goals.

Results

What can you expect from using the techniques in this chapter? Confidence and accomplishment!

You will build a clear plan that encourages you to act, and action builds confidence. Taking the first step will give you a level of confidence that will propel you toward your next step. Your confidence will be like a snowball rolling downhill, with each step and each accomplishment adding another layer of confidence.

You will get to the point where you can open yourself up for criticism, feeling good enough about yourself to be more vulnerable. Once you accept vulnerability, you will get the constructive criticism you need to improve. As you progress, you will gain more confidence and have accomplishments you didn't think were possible.

Your expectations of yourself and the people around you will change, and you will be ready to take on more and bigger challenges.

NOTES

NOTES

NOTES

PART 2

ACTION

CHAPTER 3
Put A Stake In The Ground

The phrase "putting a stake in the ground" comes from homesteading in the old west. You would stake out your claim by marking and framing land. In the last chapter, you marked your goals; now, it is time to frame the goals. You have to establish reference points to measure your progress and to give you an idea of the resources you need. Time is one of those reference points.

Time is part of the SMART goal process. The T in SMART is Time-bound. By setting an end date, you set an expectation; you put a stake in the ground. For example, I will lose 10 pounds in 60 days. An endpoint motivates you. I only have 15 days left; maybe I shouldn't have that Twinkie!

That stake in the ground is more than a motivator; it also gives you the data needed for your planning. Let's look at a multi-day hike, a 30-mile hike in which you can cover about 10 miles a day. The hike is in the wilderness, and you will need three days to finish, so you need to bring your own resources. The time you will spend in the woods determines the resources you will need.

Now you have the data and determine that you need three days of food, water, and other resources. If you only take two days' supplies, you will struggle through the last day. If you take five days' supplies, you exhaust yourself by carrying too much and you will slow yourself down. It also allows you to measure progress. Continuing the hiking analogy, you want to make sure you don't use two days of supplies on the first day. Using time to project the needs to achieve the goal accurately gives you another tool to help you succeed.

A more complex example is the goal of starting a business. Goal: In five years, I want to be working for myself. In reality, your goal will need to be more specific, but we will keep it general for the example. First, what does that mean?

1. I will be entirely responsible for my career
2. I will be my only source of income
3. I will need my own support staff

I have five years to get there. What resources do I need?

1. Income: I can't just stop everything while planning the business. I need an income
2. Time: I need to set time aside to start building the business.
3. Information: I need specific knowledge.
4. Team: I need people

Cheese Box

In martial arts, they use belts to track progress, giving people something tangible to aspire to. When you put on the white belt, you put a stake in the ground as the starting point. To oversimplify it for this example, let's call the black belt the ultimate achievement. People need to stay motivated and on track to work toward the black belt because there are exits along the way.

There are breaks at intermediate and advanced levels before you get to a black belt. We find that many students stop training at the point that enters intermediate, and then the next group leaves at the point of advanced. Surprisingly, some on the cusp of black belt quit just before they get there.

You can use the end date and work backward to determine what resources you need and when you need them; it will help you establish milestones.

When we discuss accomplishments, we often speak of milestones. Milestones are actual stone markers on a trail marking distances. Reaching milestones on the path can be exciting and a relief, particularly when you have been on a very rough part of a trail with a concern that you might be lost. Being in a dense forest with no landmarks can be unnerving, especially when you think you should have reached a milestone but have not yet. The lesson is to use your milestones as markers that show you have reached a certain point, particularly on big goals, to help keep you on the path and encourage you to push forward. When you set big goals for yourself, establish milestones to track your progress and make course corrections when required.

A mountain hike can be very challenging and can be analogous to life. There are pitfalls, beauty, accomplishments, and failures. I had a seven-and-a-half-hour hike that gave me the chance to think, challenged me to my limits, and reminded me of several lessons in achieving goals.

There was no way to replenish our resources in the woods, so planning was particularly crucial for this hike as we needed to carry water and food. Like the hike, one needs to know the destination and how to get there to achieve a goal. The challenge of bigger goals is you may not know the exact path to reach your destination. On this hike, the trails were not loops; one trail led to the next, and we needed to know which paths led back to the car. Our objective was to reach a peak over 2800 feet. We saw an opportunity to reach a second peak higher than our first (3300 feet), and we took it. It required us to change our plan and made the hike more challenging. The issue was that we did not fully orient. We were in the woods with supplies for one hike, and we decided to make the hike longer and more difficult. We were able to finish the hike, but the end was not pleasant. If you want to change your initial objective to achieve something more significant, you can. It will push you hard, but you will achieve things you did not even imagine. Have a plan but be flexible enough to adjust it to achieve your goals. When you are pushing yourself, you might find a goal more significant than your original. Go for it!

There were obstacles on our challenging trails with steep drop-offs and bear scat (poo) everywhere. Getting injured in the woods with no cellphone service can be a big problem making it essential to be attentive throughout the trip. Situational awareness is crucial, especially when you are tired. When walking through the woods, you don't want to trip over a log, slide down a steep grade or come face to face with a bear. The lesson is always to know your surroundings. Whether you are in a business meeting, in a dark parking lot, shopping at the mall, or walking in the woods, knowing your surroundings will make you more aware of pitfalls or threats.

In self-defense, they use situational awareness, but you can also apply this to goal achievement. You need to understand your surroundings and anticipate obstacles. In the OODA loop, this occurs in the Observe and Orient stages.

There are many videos online of people walking into walls or falling into fountains because their focus is entirely on their cell phones rather than watching where they were going.

What obstacles can you "walk into" because you don't have situational awareness when working on your goals:

- Increased Debt
- Legal Issues
- Relationship Problems
- Day Job in Jeopardy

You can't put blinders on; you need to be cognizant of what is happening around you as you work on achieving your goals.

Effective thinking and leadership share a common foundation, remaining calm. Challenging situations, even recreational ones like a challenging hike, can give you moments of stress. Not reaching a milestone when expected, running low on supplies, or not seeing a member of your party can be a source of anxiety. It is essential not to let the anxiety get the better of you. Even if you don't consider yourself a leader, if you can remain calm in a stressful situation, think a problem through, and execute a solution, people will follow you, and you are more likely to reach your goal. There were points on the trail where we felt lost, we were sore and tired, and it felt like the trail would not end. The lesson was to remain calm, especially when we were stressed or anxious. You can be your own worst enemy and sabotage yourself when you doubt your capabilities or are anxious about an outcome. Remain calm, think, then determine a solution to overcome your difficulties. Your objective may be right around the next bend, even if you don't see it yet.

Challenging goals can lead to anxiety. It is hard to fight your anxiety and move forward even though your target is not in sight. To achieve a challenging goal, you need to remain focused on the desired outcome. There is no giving up in the forest as to get back to civilization, you need to move forward or go back. The lesson is perseverance. In the woods, we chose to move forward, and despite being challenging, we made it. It was the right path to take (even if it did not seem so at the time).

Learning from actions taken during a project takes analysis after the project. On the ride back from our hike, we talked about what went right and what went wrong to avoid problems in the future. If you are going for a half-mile walk in the park, you don't need to go through this exercise, but if you are doing a dangerous excursion and plan on doing others, it is good to document the good and the bad. The lesson is to review it so you can learn from past mistakes and benefit from previous advantages. We learned that we need double the amount of water; we need to bring maps of the areas around our target hiking area and walkie-talkies for communication if we need to separate. We took note of these items and will make adjustments for our next excursion.

You may hear this analysis referred to as a post-mortem or an after-action report. These reports need to be honest and specific to be useful. They typically detail:

- What went right
- What went wrong
- What can be done better
- What additional things would be needed
    - Skills
    - Supplies
    - People

The milestones build a structure on which you can focus. When you have a lot of drive and are passionate about a goal, you can get excited and start acting without setting milestones. This action will set you off in every direction. You just want to act, to get closer to reaching your goal, so you tend to act on impulse.

It is like cabin fever. When you are stuck inside in the wet, cold weather, you just want to get outside and do something. We all experienced this in the COVID pandemic; the urge to rip off your mask and just go somewhere, anywhere. When it comes to your goals, we need to be more focused.

When you start a weight loss or fitness goal, you may get excited and start buying things. You may purchase workout clothes, an exercise bike, or something that makes you feel like you are working towards your goal. You can distract yourself with actions that give the appearance of moving forward, but you're just curing cabin fever, giving yourself the warm fuzzy feeling that you are doing something.

Action is the cure for the lethargy caused by not following your goals. Actions without goal-orientated focus only allow you to say you are doing something and make you feel better, but only focused effort will help you reach your objectives. Suppose you have decided to look for a job and feel motivated to take action. You look in your closet and decide you need a new suit for interviews, so you go shopping. You have taken action. The result is that you feel good, and you have rewarded yourself with a new suit. You may feel great, but have you been effective? No! Dusting off and updating your resume or reaching out to people and using your network to find what they have seen in the market would have served you better. These tasks do not have the instant gratification that buying the suit has, but they are more valuable when focusing on your goal. You need to take the time to set your stakes in the ground. What do you need to do in your job search vs. what will make you feel better?

Cheese Box

There is a scene in the movie Forest Gump where he was playing football. He is standing staring off into space until the quarterback hands him the ball and tells him to run. He takes the ball, says okay, and starts running. He avoids the defenders and scores a touchdown but continues to run out of the stadium. He had no goal; they told him to run, so he ran. The fact that he achieved the touchdown did not even come to mind.

How many of you are just running through life? Trying to get to retirement; to Friday; to five o'clock. You may have goals: sales goals and career goals, but are you just running without knowing your personal goal?

You need to determine what allows you to reach your goal more effectively.

- Does buying a new workout outfit help you get fit, or should you do some pushups?
- What has more impact, buying the suit or updating the resume for the job search?
- Will you get better results putting together an advertising campaign before a business plan?

It is essential to act with intention. Putting stakes in the ground is the way to plan with purpose. You determine the importance of what you need to do so you don't go off chasing shiny things. Advertisers are experts at getting you to chase shiny things. You see weight loss ads when you make your new year's resolutions. You see companies that will help you sell your products; all you need to do is buy their products. It is pervasive. You do some online research, and suddenly you are inundated with advertisements that sell the product to solve all of your problems. To paraphrase the Grinch, "Maybe your goals don't come from the store; maybe your goals mean a little bit more."

Looking for shortcuts to success is smart, and we should all work smarter rather than harder. However, be cautious that you have found a shortcut and not a distraction (products or actions) disguising itself as productive action.

It is effortless to fool yourself that you are working toward your goals when you are merely distracting yourself in reality. How many times have you heard people say that they cannot lose weight no matter how hard they try? Losing weight is simple but not easy. It is simple because if you live with a calorie deficit (you burn more calories than you consume), you will lose weight. It is not easy because high-calorie food options that appear to be healthy are all around us. If you don't prioritize cooking your food, you will eat processed foods. Exercise routines do not burn as many calories as you think, so you overeat. Someone sent me a meme that said the only way to burn 800 calories in a half-hour is to put a pizza in the oven at 450 degrees for the half-hour.

The most crucial stake in the ground is the starting line. You need to execute and take the first step, or nothing will get done.

It seems so simple; you need to get to work, but you are so distracted and stressed out that you tend to let the starting point slide. How many times have you postponed a task or a goal because you weren't ready? You make serious plans, and you think you are working, but you are delaying. You start using delaying tactics instead of actual work, like buying workout clothes to prepare for exercise or making lists of prospects but not making any calls.

When you are starting a very challenging goal, the most difficult move is the first. When I was a kid, I needed to dive from a diving platform. It was not the highest, but it looked pretty high to me. It was my goal, and the process was simple; walk up the ladder, position myself on the platform, dive into the pool. This example demonstrates that simple does not mean easy. I had a fear of heights.

When I was told I needed to dive from the diving board, I did a lot of preparation.

- I surveyed the equipment
- I did some warm-ups
- (when pushed to act) I went and tested the ladder

- I climbed the ladder and surveyed the platform from the ladder
- (when pushed to act) I went to the diving position
- I considered all of my diving options (I only knew one)
- (when pushed to act) I dove into the pool

How many of those steps were necessary?

- It was a concrete platform. Did it need to be inspected?
- The dive was a warm-up. Did I need a pre-warm-up warm-up?

The gym teacher was the third party who pushed me to go. I was succumbing to my fear rather than planning and preparing. You do this with your goals; you warm up when warmed up and survey equipment that does not need to be surveyed. If it weren't for that gym teacher, I think I would still be testing the ladder. After the first dive, when I realized that I wouldn't die doing it, I was able just to go up and dive.

That was my first step toward my conquering my fear of heights. This story shows the use of milestones and the importance of accountability. I held myself accountable, even if it was because I did not want to look weak in front of my classmates. There was a third party holding me accountable. There were milestones – ladder, platform, dive.

Milestones and accountability are vital factors in achieving your goals. Again, it is simple, but it is not easy. I have had many goals that died at the end of the planning period because I did not hold myself accountable. It is easy to keep saying that you will stay on track, but you tend to move your stakes until they fit your narrative that you are achieving your goals.

Here is a partial list of milestones that I never hit because I did not hold myself accountable:

- I took a voiceover class but never followed up
- Speaking for a living
- Starting a business
- Opening a martial arts school
- Participating in a triathlon

Can you identify goals that died at the end of the planning period because you were distracted or did not act?

I have worked on my public speaking. I have competed at a national level in speaking competitions and have spoken to groups from 10 to near 1000. I did this 20+ years ago. I had the opportunity to and took classes on using my voice to earn money. I set myself up for success with two primary income-producing paths, speaking and voice-overs. Using a football analogy, I was at the five-yard line. Then I got "realistic."

1. I needed to build up a little more capital before I started.
2. I should get a bit more work experience to build credibility
3. Work just got busier. I will start in six months
4. Insert new excuses here until the goals are unachieved and in the rearview mirror.

These were not obstacles; I did not try to conquer these issues. They were excuses I used not to start. There are things I could have done to get started.

1. I did not need to quit my job to start. I could have had my income and started the business.
2. I had credibility. I was insecure and ended up stalling rather than overcoming my insecurity.
3. Successful people are always busy. I had plenty of time to achieve my goals. I was just filling that time with distractions.
4. I had a lot of other excuses. The bottom line, I was afraid and moved my goals to fit my small thinking.

I had the opportunity, but I let 20 years pass. Many people would say I waited too long, but here we are. I wrote the book, you are reading it, and I am speaking to groups. It is not too late for me to achieve my goals, and it is not too late for you to achieve yours.

My first book, "Late Bloomer, It's not too late to succeed!" is also a project 20+ years in the making. I wrote a book 23 years ago and am not sure where that manuscript is. I got right to the finish line, and I stopped before I crossed. I left that book so far in the rearview mirror that I did not even think about it until today, writing this section. I now have about 20 book ideas that are sitting in a file box. (Yes, I actually write my thoughts with pen and paper. I drive my wife nuts with all the notebooks I have). You might see some of those ideas in future books. How many ideas do you have in file cabinets or on shelves? What is holding you back? Why aren't you starting?

The delay in my book included a little fear but was more of a lack of discipline. I did not put a firm stake in the ground. I would write regularly for a week and then get distracted. I would read what I wrote and get stuck in the mud, trying to edit chapter one before I even had a picture of the end result. I would pick it up a month later for a day or two, and then all of a sudden, it is a year later, and I would come across the notes when looking for another one of my ideas. It is easy to lose yourself over time.

I have other stories on almost getting there; working toward my goal, and then:

- "look, there's a shiny thing."
- Fear tells me I'm not ready.
- Work gets too "busy."

Who's to blame for all of these delays and false starts? There is only one villain in my story: that's me!

- I prioritized the shiny thing over my goals
- I succumbed to my fear
- I convinced myself that I was too busy.

We all encounter distractions and self-doubt. When you are putting a stake in the ground, look closely at what is happening around you.

- What is your shiny thing? Do you want to lose weight? What is more important, the cupcakes from your coworker or your weight loss goals?
- We all have fear. What can you do to overcome those fears? Take action! Do something. Remember, after my first dive, I was able to continue without fear.
- Are you really too busy? How much TV do you watch? When I measured my time, I found two hours in the morning, 6:00 AM to 8:00 AM, while getting ready for work and 7:00 PM to 11:00 PM, another four hours.

That is six hours a day! Every workweek (Monday to Friday) is THIRTY HOURS! I had an extra 30 hours a week! How many hours do you have?

When I stopped lying to myself about the amount of time I have, I found that I can still watch TV, have downtime and do family things, but I can achieve my objectives while working full time. I put stakes firmly in the ground, hold myself accountable, and employ people I trust to hold me accountable.

You can achieve your biggest, craziest goals by doing this. Five years ago, writing one book would have been an insane goal for me, never mind a second book. Look at your goals, set your milestones, and see what you can accomplish!

"Play like you're in first. Train like you're in second."
— STEPHEN CURRY

Reflection

Are you prepared to strive for your goals? Take out your journal. Take each of your goals and work backward to where you are today. Look at each milestone. Are there interim steps to reach each milestone?

Stake out your claim! Frame your goals with milestones. Things will come up that disrupt your plans but having a step-by-step plan can keep you on track. No goal journey is a straight line.

Compare your plan to a cross-country drive. You could measure the number of miles you need to travel, estimate the number of miles you need to cover each day and set a series of milestones between your starting and endpoints. Suppose you have car trouble in the middle of your trip; you will need to adjust your plan. There may be weather issues, road construction, or any other obstacles that could pop up along the way, so you need to be flexible. Your overall plan provides the structure necessary to stay on track.

Have you ever used milestones (for example, a long drive)? How has it kept you on track?

Takeaways

You have prepared yourself, and it is time to go to work. You want to make sure that you are working towards your goals. You have spent the time planning and preparing yourself; it would be a shame to lose momentum now. You need to move, but you need to be disciplined.

To be successful and reach your full potential, you need to work with intention.

To achieve your goals and progress beyond where you are now, you need to understand why you are doing something. Once you know why you are doing something, you have the base for improvement. I knew of a company that had the process to receive a delivery of parts that was put into storage, waiting for another part. Someone asked, "why?" It turned out that it had always been done that way. At some stage, the manufacturing process had changed, but the delivery process did not. The company was able to save money and staffing by updating the delivery schedule.

Knowing why you are doing a task is one of the techniques we worked on when preparing yourself. You were getting ready for the starting line. If you have ever watched a drag race, you'd have seen the cars spinning their tires as they approach the starting line. They are heating their tires to improve traction. They are preparing to start just like we are.

By identifying the starting line, you have put your first stake in the ground. You are approaching the point where you can measure results. If you don't measure, you never really know where you stand. When you don't measure, you tend to exaggerate your results. Adding a bit of wishful thinking mixed with feelings that you worked hard and believe you deserve a particular outcome, so you lie to yourself.

Putting stakes in the ground to challenge yourself and having a matrix to measure yourself against is integral to reaching your potential. It can also be a great ego booster, as achieving wins along the way keep you motivated.

You need to keep out eye on the prize as you strive to achieve your goals, knowing that the ultimate stake in the ground is at goal achievement. You have a start and finish line. What can you use to keep you on track from the start through the finish?

Results

You now have a framework to scale your goals. You can accomplish goals even though you can't see the finish line. You can focus, get rid of your excuses, and effectively achieve big goals.

Let's say you are working in the mailroom, and your objective is to become company president. You can use milestones to frame your goal and take steps that you can measure.

Milestones

1. Mailroom clerk → work hard → promoted to Mailroom Manager
2. Mailroom Manager → get accounting degree → Accountant
3. Accountant → study reports → Finance Manager
4. Finance Manager → build people skills → Head Business Development
5. Business Development → build product knowledge → Head Operations
6. Head of Operations → build executive skills → President

This example is simplified, but this framework will put you in a position to achieve your biggest goals. What are you going to do today to get started?

NOTES

NOTES

NOTES

CHAPTER 4
Overcome Your Obstacles

You understand your definition of success, you've set your goals, you know where you are now, you've established a plan to achieve your goals, decided to start, and are taking action. Wow, you are on your way to achievement, and bang, you hit your first obstacle. What do you do? Do you stop, or do you move forward? You will hit obstacles, so you need to figure out what you will do when encountering them.

When you get off track with your goal, you can punish yourself for making excuses. A great example is a weight loss goal. Many, like me, struggle with weight issues, bouncing back and forth in an endless cycle of gaining and losing weight. Do you fail because you make excuses? It can be true as we all have excuses. For example, you have a tough day, so you skip the gym. Instead, you have a cheat day, eating junk food and drinking beer. However, labeling all setbacks as excuses is doing yourself a disservice and will only discourage you. We all have genuine obstacles that may hinder our goals.

There are obstacles that you may need to conquer when you are striving to achieve a goal. Continuing with the weight loss goal as an example:

- Slower metabolism due to excess fat
- Joint pain due to excess weight
- Having to drive kids around when you had planned to go to the gym
- Having to go to a business dinner
- People bringing food to work

These are all obstacles, but not reasons to give up. It would be best if you considered these things when setting your goals. It means recognizing them and addressing them. Using the OODA loop, you can overcome these obstacles.

- Example 1 – <u>Observe</u>: I am not losing weight as fast as I used to. <u>Orient</u>: My metabolism is slower. <u>Decide</u>: I need a more significant calorie deficit. <u>Act</u>: Reduce calorie intake, and increase workouts.
- Example 2 – <u>Observe</u>: My knees hurt. <u>Orient</u>: My weight is hindering my performance. <u>Decide</u>: I need lower impact exercises. <u>Act</u>: Start with low impact exercises and work up to more challenging workouts
- Example 3 – <u>Observe</u>: Kids needed a ride <u>Orient</u>: I had to miss my gym appointment <u>Decide</u>: I need to schedule my exercise better <u>Act</u>: Go to the gym early in the morning
- Example 4 – <u>Observe</u>: I have to meet a client for dinner <u>Orient</u>: Ordering a salad will distract from the sale <u>Decide</u>: I will order a traditional dinner that doesn't set

me back. <u>Act</u>: Order dinner light on carbs and make up for it tomorrow

- Example 5 – <u>Observe</u>: People brought high-calorie food to work <u>Orient</u>: I will hurt their feelings if I don't eat the food. <u>Decide</u>: I need to eat not to alienate people or destroy my diet. <u>Act</u>: Take a small portion.

It is not easy to overcome obstacles. When your coworker brings in their best dish for everyone, it is hard to say no. There is the willpower factor that you want to eat the high-calorie food, but there is also the pressure you feel from your coworkers and the need to bond and maintain the relationships you've built. If someone brings in bagels or leftover birthday cake, there is no emotion in it, and you can skip it. If someone brings in a dish that they obviously spent a long time preparing and are excited for you to eat, it is prudent to make an exception.

Only you can decide if something is an excuse or an obstacle. I like to use the example of a coworker bringing bagels to the office. I love bagels. When I have a bagel, I will not rip out the middle and put a teaspoon of low-fat cream cheese on it. When I want a bagel, I am going all in. That means that I need to be strategic when having a bagel and doing it on my terms.

Being a stress eater, I know that if I give in to the bagel in the morning, I will give in again and have another one when I walk by the kitchen after a stressful meeting. That is why I need to put the stake in the ground in the morning and politely decline. It is funny how we struggle mentally with the first, but the second is easier. I know that if I gave in and had one, I would rationalize in the afternoon, "well, I already screwed up today;

I might as well have another and start fresh tomorrow." When we open the door to excuses, it is easy to justify the excuses.

Again, avoid confusing excuses with obstacles. Obstacles are real. If you blame your willpower for missing the gym when you had to drive the kids around, you are doing yourself a disservice. In this case, missing the gym is not an excuse. It is a mistake in your planning or just bad luck.

I was supposed to go to my martial arts class last week; I was all set with my gi (uniform) in the car. I planned well, I had my work completed for the day, and I was ready to go. Then I got a text message that threw those plans into disarray.

The windshield of my son's car had a crack; we'd scheduled to have it fixed that day. For once the windshield replacement company was on time, they took the moldings off of the windshield, started to loosen it up, and it started to sleet. The technician wasn't allowed to work in inclement weather; he stopped and left. It left us with an unusable car and multiple people that needed to go places. I needed to step in and drive people around.

My missing class was not an excuse. It was an obstacle. Of course, I had a choice. I could have said that the kids had to find their own way to work or that my wife had to find her way to her meeting. I completed the OODA loop. Observe: We're short of a car. Orient: People would miss income-earning opportunities if I did not provide transportation. Decide: Their jobs had a higher priority than my class. Act: Skip class and drive kids.

Now, if my kids had dates or were going to hang out with friends, they would have been out of luck. My martial arts class would have been a higher priority in my Orient stage than going to the mall. Since they were going to work, they got a higher priority.

In general, there are three ways to deal with obstacles.

1. Address the obstacle – Meet the obstacle head-on and overcome it.
2. Avoid the obstacle – Design your path so you do not encounter the obstacle
3. Accept the obstacle – Some obstacles can't be addressed or avoided. For example, I have had five knee surgeries. I will never be a top runner, but I can still enjoy running a 5K road race.

There are self-imposed and external obstacles. How you handle them differs.

Obstacles that you erect for yourself can be behaviors that compensate for gaps in your life. These behaviors can be unhealthy eating or smoking; it can be procrastination; it can be accepting unfair treatment. Whatever it is, there is a gap in your life that you need to fill. You need to be careful in identifying the cause of the gap, as we all tend to project the effects of the real problem onto a more convenient target. You may work in a toxic work environment that puts you under stress at work, and it can affect your marriage or family. It is easy to blame your marriage and family for your discomfort since they are easy targets even though the real problem is the toxic work environment.

If you don't address the gaps in your life, you will constantly feel like something is missing or off. I think of it as a shopping cart with a bad wheel. Selecting a shopping cart is mindless; you just grab one without any thought. If it is a smooth ride, you keep going. If it has a bad wheel, thunk, thunk, thunk, you might get another one. What you do depends on your mood. The cart might only have a minor problem, so you think you will deal with it. Have you ever been tired in a crowded store, stressed out, just want your shopping done, and get the cart with THUNK, THUNK, THUNK? It is so loud, you think everyone around you can hear it, but you just deal with it even though it jars you to your core and increases your stress level as you shop.

That is how I see self-imposed obstacles. You have the opportunity to change them. Initially, they are a little annoying, but you deal with it. If it gets out of hand, you recognize the obstacle and work to get over it. It is when you are stressed out, overwhelmed, and tired that you merely accept the discomfort. The discomforting gap becomes a constant presence, a feeling lingering in the background, a continuous negative rhythm affecting your life. You can feel it somewhere in your subconscious, but you try to ignore it or feel powerless to address it.

Cheese Box

There are consequences for not overcoming internal obstacles:

1. Excess weight – being overweight slows you down, steals your energy, leaves you open to health issues, and changes how people look at you.
2. Unhealthy Habits – Unhealthy eating and drinking can affect your attention. Addictive behaviors can lead you to make bad decisions, and you can look uninterested or weak to your peers.

3. Stigma-causing behaviors – Drug abuse and criminal behavior can lead to incarceration that can limit your opportunities to succeed.
4. Stagnating – If you aren't growing, you are dying. People can see if you are not growing. As others progress, you will be left behind.

These internal obstacles interfere with achieving your goals, but they are within your control to change. The term "in your control" does not mean that you can overcome your obstacle by yourself. Many self-imposed obstacles require other people's support to overcome. When I reference control, I mean you have the power to make the decision. All the people in the world can be ready to help, but if you don't choose to make the change, no one can help you.

Just as a reminder, obstacles are not reasons to fail; they are challenges to overcome. An example is the significant stress hitting young people applying for college admission. Some kids don't do well in high school, which can be a massive obstacle to college admission. For students who have academic challenges, college can seem out of reach. The community college system in the state I live offers preparatory courses. These courses are not credit courses, but they allow the students to learn the skills needed to succeed in college for those who did do well enough in high school. They do not reject the students that don't achieve the minimum on admittance tests. They get to learn the skills they need to overcome their obstacles, giving them a better chance to succeed. When the student finishes the two-year program, they are prepared for a four year college and can apply the courses they've taken toward graduating from four-year colleges that would not have considered them when they graduated high school.

It would help if you did the same thing for yourself. You need to give yourself those preparatory steps to overcome your self-imposed obstacles to move forward. Luckily, you can overcome many of these obstacles while you strive forward; however, you may need to address some first. For example, you will need to get into recovery first if you have a substance abuse problem. If you have been incarcerated, you will need to serve your time first. If you don't have the energy for a second job, you need first to address your health.

Overcoming obstacles is more challenging in isolation. There are some obstacles you can't overcome without other people. Everyone wants to be strong and independent, a desire propagated by Pop culture and your influencers. Boys are told, "Be your own man." Women are told, "You don't need anyone." Both statements are true. Men and women can be strong and independent. However, we have taken the concept too far. Being strong and independent does not mean being isolated.

I have resisted being vulnerable and would typically address obstacles with blunt force, attacking the problem and doing things myself, not seeking out help. When I did go for help, I would not fully open myself, so I would not get the full benefit of my team's assistance. I was fooling myself that I was getting help, but I was just going through the motions. In the past (to be honest, I am still struggling with it), I did not think a strong, independent person could be vulnerable. It wasn't until I read Brené Brown's "Daring Greatly" that I started to understand the role of vulnerability in overcoming obstacles.

I benefited from my coaching and mentor relationships, but I gained so much more when I became vulnerable and opened my mind to new possibilities.

To recap, to overcome self-imposed obstacles, you need to:

- recognize you have obstacles (Observe)
- see how the obstacles affect you (Orient)
- determine how you will address the obstacles (Decide)
- get the support you need and overcome the obstacle (Act)

What are some common obstacles that you have?

- Ego – I have heard the ego described as an airbag. When you are in an accident, it protects us, but it blocks the road from your view when it is open all the time. Your egos can blind you to the benefits of getting help from others. In martial arts, many black belts experience resistance to vulnerability. They feel they are above taking classes, which is when they start performing poorly. In life, as in martial arts, to advance, you need more growth, not less. You need to move beyond your ego and keep learning.
- Fear of missing out – Fear can paralyze us. Fear of missing something can get you stuck in planning, keeping you on a losing path. I know a business owner that has a paralyzing fear of missing out. He is wealthy and does not trust his employees. Instead of giving them some control, he let thousands of assets lose value because he never dealt with them.
- Lack of trust – the example above also highlights this point. You should not trust blindly, so build a team of people you can work with and help one another succeed. To reach your full potential, you need to scale your efforts.

- Jealousy of others' achievements – If you are discouraged by other people's accomplishments and dwell on how you view their success, you won't have the energy to work on your goals. Be inspired by others' success. If they succeeded, so can you.

Life would be simpler if you only encountered internal obstacles. However, many obstacles are outside your control. Suppose you have a crucial meeting two hours away and there is a bad snowstorm; you don't have any control over the weather. You need to deal with it. Because there is nothing you can do to change the weather, your options are to leave the day before and get a hotel, reschedule the meeting or set up a video conference.

External obstacles can be easier to face than internal obstacles. It is easier to visualize the snowstorm than the bad choices that made you 50 pounds too heavy. However, you can have difficulty overcoming external obstacles. How you dealt with your internal obstacles will affect how you deal with external obstacles. Having energy, good self-esteem, a strong team, and a good attitude will put you in a better position to conquer these.

Use the OODA loop to overcome your external obstacles. Solving problems demonstrates the difference between simple and easy. The OODA loop is simple, but solving problems is not easy. Overcoming internal and external obstacles have the same process. You just handle the internal obstacles first because they are obstacles to overcome external obstacles.

What are some of the obstacles that many will face?

- Toxic Company Cultures - Working in a negative environment can damage your self-esteem and hurt your ability to get ahead not just in that company but also in other endeavors. You either need to insulate yourself from the toxicity or leave the company.
- Economic Activity – If there is an economic downturn, you can lose your job or have trouble finding new opportunities.
- Family Issues – A family crisis can require a change of plan and may need you to postpone or change your approach to achieving your goals.

Overcoming obstacles can be a great or an awful experience, depending on your approach. I had opportunities to participate in obstacle races, and each was a completely different experience based on my approach.

In my first race, I completed it myself. As I had never done an obstacle race, I did not know what to expect. I watched a few YouTube videos but didn't talk to anyone who had done one before, and I did not prepare. I entered the race completely unprepared and without a plan; it was not a pleasant experience. I remember finishing a particularly challenging obstacle, grabbing a water bottle from the station, and hearing a volunteer yell, keep going; you're halfway there. I kept going, and then it struck me. Am I only halfway through? After the obstacles I had just been through and now considering having to do the same or worse to finish daunted me. I felt like I was lost in the woods with no exit. I saw no path to move forward. The next obstacle was to walk up a ski slope carrying a weighted bag; I wanted to walk off the course and quit. I opted to move forward, I took a lot of breaks, but I made it through.

I overcame the obstacles. It was miserable, but I accomplished my goal.

We talked about obstacle races at work about a year later, so I gave a rose-colored version of my experience. (remember, we want people to accept and respect us, so we tend to change the story to meet the situation). This motivated people in my company to form a team. We trained, we supported each other, and we learned about the race.

We got to the race, pumped each other up, ran the race together, supporting each other through the obstacles. We had a great time, and all finished. The time was much better than when I did alone.

What was the difference?

1. I had done it before, knowing it was achievable helped a lot
2. We researched the obstacles, and we had a better idea of how to tackle them
3. We had a team. The support of other people is key to being able to achieve your goals.

My experiences in the obstacle races apply to any obstacle you are encountering. Let's say you are out of work and are looking for a job.

Situation 1: You are alone in your house searching the want ads online. You are not sure what employers need in new employees. You haven't written a resume in ten years.

Situation 2: You are working with a job search group that brings together people in transition. You are talking to your network about potential jobs, and you are taking a free resume writing class at your library.

Which situation sounds better? When you're faced with an unexpected obstacle, you can act like a wounded bear and retreat to your den and roar at anyone who approaches. Retreating into your metaphorical cave is an instinct you need to fight. Face the obstacle, be vulnerable enough to ask for and to accept help, and work to overcome that obstacle.

Overcoming obstacles is not easy. Using the OODA loop is simple. Use the simple path to overcome the difficult obstacle.

Reflection

What obstacles are you facing right now? Are your obstacles internal or external?

List your obstacles in your journal and consider their source. Once documented, you can determine how you are going to overcome them. Use the OODA Loop to detail your plan and to act on overcoming each obstacle.

You may find commonalities with your obstacles, and by eliminating certain behaviors or leaving certain situations, you may overcome multiple obstacles at once.

Prioritize your obstacles. Which obstacles should you attack first? Typically, eliminating internal obstacles will put you in a better position to attack your external obstacles.

Takeaways

Obstacles are not excuses. They are real, but you can handle them.

Address the obstacle – Overweight? Lose weight.

Avoid the obstacle – Can't get into a four-year college from high school? Go to community college first.

Accept the obstacle – You are getting older? It is better than the alternative.

Obstacles are part of your path to success.

Put effort into identifying your obstacles.

Results

Using the techniques in this chapter will allow you to build a positive, challenging environment. You have control over your attitude. You can choose how you respond to obstacles.

Taking action is satisfying. You will find happiness in the work. Once you shed the fear of missing out and accept that life is a team sport, you will be happy working toward your goals. Life is a journey. Opening yourself up, being vulnerable, mitigating your fear, and developing the OODA Loop habit will help you live the life you are meant to live!

NOTES

NOTES

NOTES

CHAPTER 5
Execution In The Face Of Uncertainty

You have put a stake in the ground, you are dealing with your obstacles, but it can still be challenging to keep moving toward your goals. When you are working toward your goals, anything can happen, and the biggest hurdle you have to face is uncertainty. You can get hit by a meteor. It's unlikely, but it is possible. Your imagination can uncover the craziest consequences if you make a mistake. If you are going to succeed, you must act despite uncertainties.

A good example is my writing. I published my first book even though I was no expert in publishing. If a book is your goal, writing is only the first step in the publishing process. There is so much you still need to do once you have written the book. I did not know any of that when I started writing. I just wrote and did not worry about any of the other tasks because until you have a book draft, the rest doesn't matter.

Writers have dreams of best sellers and people seeking them out. Unless you are a celebrity, this is not the reality; you need to do most of the legwork yourself to promote your book. I did not know that and imagined that I would have more support.

Since I had no idea how this process worked, I had to make a decision.

Let's use the OODA Loop to demonstrate how I made and acted on my decision.

Observe: As I was writing, I networked to find the experts and reached out to get introductions to people I needed to for information. I sourced as much information as I could.

Orient: With my experience and network, I needed to invest more time to get the book marketed fully. I also had the option to use the book to improve my personal brand, learn what authors need to do when the book is complete, and be a coach.

Decide: I decided to use the book to improve my personal brand and learn what authors do beyond writing.

Act: I have been leveraging the first book to improve my personal brand and showcase my skills as a coach and speaker.

With that information, I changed how I used the book. Instead of the book being the product, I used the book to increase and enhance my personal brand.

I chose to use the book as a marketing tool for my personal brand. Some people give their book away for marketing, and I am not doing that. I still sell the book; it is both a product and a tool, a vital part of the Chad C. Betz product line. That product line includes my day job, the book, and any coaching or consulting I do on the side.

These were all things I learned along the way. I spoke to a best-selling author on how I should market the book. I talked to an author who uses the book as a tool for his business. I spoke to the owner of one of the top independent bookstores in America.

I talked to people who self-published. They all contributed to my plan by adding their experience, which enhanced mine and helped me succeed. I continue to learn as I go, but I did not let uncertainty become an obstacle. Using the advice from experts who had done this before, I became the second mouse.

The process is never perfect. You will miss some steps, you will learn, and you will compensate. In my process, I learned that an author should start publicizing their book for around six months before publishing. The problem was that I learned this a month after publishing my book.

Learning something after you have committed can be a point of distress. You may feel it is a catastrophic screw-up and want to stop working. When I realized I had skipped a vital step, I felt that pressure. I thought that I didn't know what I was doing. I questioned myself, "What was I thinking trying to publish on my own? How could I have missed this?"

I reflected on my mistakes and talked to my coach. I had to step back and think about the real impact of acting in an environment of uncertainty. The goal of my book was to improve my personal brand. How was that going?

1. I am a published author. That is a positive
2. People were buying my book. That is a positive
3. People were coming to my presentations. That is a positive
4. I learned that I could get even more publicity for future projects if I started publicizing before publishing. That is a positive.

Could I have had more success if I started publicizing before I published? Maybe. However, if I worried about every potential scenario, I would have never published my book, so it would not have mattered. I worked in an environment of uncertainty, and I published a book. I used what I learned from the first book to publish this book, eliminating some of the uncertainty. There are traps throughout the process. As you learn, and as you see, there is more to learn, giving you the feeling that you need to stop and not move forward. You need to have faith, to believe in yourself and your goals.

> *"Leap, and the net will appear."*
>
> — JOHN BURROUGHS

Dealing with uncertainty does not mean flying blind. I once had a job opportunity with a high-income potential, and I took the job without the proper research. A bank hired me to head a mortgage department in a new branch. I hit the ground running and started networking with local businesses and high influence people. I built relationships and was ready to go. The bank board voted against opening the branch. I was still assigned to the area, but the nearest office was over 10 miles away. With all the competition, it was hard to get traction without a local brick-and-mortar location. Since there was no new branch in their area, the local business people and influencers lost interest, leaving me hanging.

I disregarded uncertainty when making my decision. I did not know that the board had not voted on the branch. If I did, I would have asked more questions. Now, whose fault is it that I did not know? It was ultimately my fault. I should have asked more questions, but instead, I saw dollar signs, and the president's enthusiasm was infectious. I did not think about what I did not know, and the information I had led me to believe it could have been a big success. With a few more questions, I could have avoided almost a year of digging into my savings and building up debt. It took me four years to recover financially, and my confidence was shaken. Even to this day, I tend to get a little too gun-shy when I look at opportunities.

Opportunities will arise, and some may seem great. They may be presented by people you respect and trust, and it is easy to get infected by their enthusiasm and forget that you do not have all the information you need to make a decision. It is essential to consider all of the available facts while understanding that you will never have all the facts. Sometimes time does not allow you to analyze an opportunity thoroughly, so you need to balance the risk and the return. The risk includes the impact your decision will have on those around you and future prospects. You need to analyze as much as possible without being crippled by not having all of the information. Jumping into the wrong opportunity can have a long-reaching impact on your life, so analyze the risk and decide accordingly.

You have to act with some uncertainty, but you shouldn't just jump at an opportunity without research. Taking action in an environment of uncertainty does not mean being lazy about asking questions. I clouded the reality of the opportunity with my hopes and dreams of the ideal result and was lazy about asking questions. Get as much information as possible, and don't get stuck in the hamster wheel trap of getting "all the information." You need to balance your risk mitigation and your ability to act in uncertainty

You may not be jumping at opportunities, and you may not be stuck in planning. You may just be stuck not knowing what to do. My industry has been flattening for the last decade, causing many colleagues to find jobs in other sectors or take positions that are not an ideal fit. I am fortunate to have stayed in the industry and maintain positions at which I have been successful. Because there are fewer opportunities, I am unsure if I should stay in the industry or move to another.

After more than 20 years in my industry, I have had fun and learned a lot. Inertia tells me not to throw away my 20 years of experience. On the positive side, I can add a lot of value with my industry knowledge and achieve my goals if I am patient.

Another choice is to leverage the skills I've accumulated and apply them to a new industry with more opportunities. That is a scary prospect. Some of those who've made this transition were forced into it after being laid off. With nothing available in their industry of choice, and were forced to consider alternatives. A change like this takes time and is hard work. Some are happy to be working, but others have found their calling, receiveng more satisfaction than their previous careers.

I am unsure if I am impatient and that my opportunity will come in this industry or if my industry has contracted to the point that options have been exhausted. Inertia keeps me in this industry, but curiosity and ambition keep me considering other industries.

I am still working through what I want to do. I believe in consistent reflection. As you change over time, so do your needs. As you reflect and consider opportunities, you can decide what you want to do. It is more than just blindly following your passion. I enjoy writing and public speaking, but realistically I can't afford just to write and give speeches right now. I need to have a day job.

You are accountable for your goals, and here, you cannot have uncertainty; you need to have clarity. To recap on having clarity on your goals, review chapters one and two. You are accountable for your success, and there are several ways to hold yourself accountable; you don't need to do it alone. Accountability is essential for milestones. If you are not held accountable, you will slide on your goals

I worked for a company that did not fire people. A few employees did not produce, especially one assigned to my team when the company hired me. He focused on food more than work. He would arrive just on time and go to the kitchen area to prepare breakfast, including slicing fruit and other time-consuming activities. He would sit at the conference table to eat his breakfast before starting work. Around 11:00, he would ask colleagues about lunch. After gathering lunch orders, he would disappear for an hour or so before coming back with lunch. He would take another break in the afternoon but still leave on time.

I observed this for a couple of days before chatting to my boss, who acknowledged that this employee needed to change, as he had been acting this way for five years. My boss asked me to coach him to get him on track. Having worked this way for so long made him a weak candidate for coaching, and he became the first person in the company's history to be fired. This action woke up many other workers. I held people accountable, making them realize that they needed to perform to not be in jeopardy.

A lack of accountability leads to many taking the path of least resistance. If we do not have career goals or if we do, and we don't hold ourselves accountable, we go to work; we work; we go home. If we have weight loss goals and don't hold ourselves accountable, we will slip.

Personal accountability is the most important. If you have not committed, it does not matter who else has committed. In our earlier example, our food-obsessed employee was not committed to change. I spent weeks focused on getting him on track. I brought him to a conference, so he and I could have face time outside the office. I coached him on preparing his food at home to get more work done when he was working. He was resistant to any change.

Why wouldn't he be resistant? He'd done this for years and was given raises and bonuses for working like this. When you reward bad behavior, you can't expect a good response. He had no reason to hold himself accountable for his career.

If you have goals to achieve, you have to hold yourself accountable. For my weight loss, I have many third parties helping to hold me accountable. There are doctors, my family, and others that want me to lose weight. Because my focus was on other things, I have not put enough commitment into my weight loss.

Between writing this book, preparing a two-hour goal-setting seminar, other projects I am working on, and having a full-time job, I had to choose one set of objectives over another. Having multiple goals that are time intensive can create situations when your goals become your obstacles. It is a known fact that busy people get the most done. The more active you get, the more focused you need to be. As you get more done and burn through the low-hanging fruit, you need to hold yourself even more accountable.

Having so much to do does not mean I can't lose weight and saying I can't lose weight because I am busy is an excuse. Recognizing that being busy makes it more difficult to lose weight is recognizing it as an obstacle that I need to overcome by being more efficient with my time. I need to make it a priority and hold myself accountable.

Personal accountability is vital but does not diminish the value of third-party accountability. My doctor pushing and reminding me that I have the opportunity to drop the maintenance medications and be healthier, and my son asking, "see you at the gym today, dad?" help me to hold myself accountable.

I had a personal trainer in the past, and I am signing up with her again as I need her guidance and a plan to help me achieve my goals. She then holds me accountable. Having the full spread of accountability is what I need. I have the doctor I see a couple of times a year (not enough for milestone accountability). It is too easy to forget him, but he has the authority, and I remember when I take my maintenance meds. My trainer gives me a plan to stick to and holds me accountable. I have my son reminding me, and he is most helpful when I have decided and I am on the edge of going or not; his asking gives me the little nudge I need to put the laptop down and work out for an hour.

Third-party accountability alone will do nothing but annoy you. However, if you commit and start holding yourself accountable, third-party accountability can be a great tool.

At the beginning of the process, you are motivated and excited to be doing something new, and you hold yourself accountable. As the process moves along, you can lose motivation. When motivation wanes, third-party accountability, like my doctor saying that I will drop the cholesterol medication or my son asking if I will join him at the gym, can help. Those are the little kicks in the butt that help maintain accountability.

Reflection

Do you have projects or goals that you have not started because of uncertainty?

Are you asking enough questions and not getting trapped by uncertainty if you aren't getting all of the answers?

Look at your journal. What goals are you ignoring? What can you do today to get you on track to achieving that goal? If you don't have the information you need to mitigate your risk, what can you do today to get that information?

Are you holding yourself accountable? How can you make yourself more accountable for achieving your goals?

Takeaways

You will never have all of the information you need to act on your goals. You need to have risk mitigation strategies to get as much information as possible and then move forward.

You can't have uncertainty with your goals. Review part one.

Hold yourself accountable and get others to hold you accountable. Without accountability for each milestone, you are permitting yourself not to achieve your goals.

Results

The whole world is within your grasp when you accept risk. You will achieve goals more significant than you can imagine when you open yourself up to calculated risk. Not every risk will pay off; you will make mistakes, and learning from those mistakes will bring you closer to your goals. You will feel empowered when you take responsibility for those mistakes, and the lessons will build your confidence.

Commit to your goals, take calculated risks, recognize mistakes as part of the process. It is how you will achieve your goals!

NOTES

NOTES

NOTES

PART 3

RELATIONSHIPS

CHAPTER 6
The Importance Of Relationships

Life is a team sport. You are happier and more successful when you are part of an effective team. At first glance, because of experiences as kids or work life, you may not be open to viewing teamwork as a positive. We have experienced group projects at school, where a couple of team members had to carry lazy members to ensure a good grade. Many have also had the experience where one or two people name themselves leaders and try to push everyone to do the project their way. This aversion to teams continues when you experience ineffective teams in the office.

For your goals, you get to choose your team. You can build stronger relationships with people who can help you and eliminate people who tend to hinder your progress. Unfortunately, you need to overcome some obstacles when developing your teams.

I know someone whose job straddles sales and analytics. His main job is to source transactions, and his secondary responsibility is to complete a cursory analysis of the transaction to determine if it is worth pursuing. His fear of rejection leads him to talk to the same people, get access to deals that everyone else in the industry has access to, and focus on the analysis.

He works hard and wants to succeed but is confused about why his performance is mediocre. He hides behind his analytics work, putting himself in a position where it is impossible to achieve his goals. This person is a great case study because he genuinely believes he is doing his best, and he is unwilling to try new things.

By building a wall with his analytics work, he prevents himself from truly succeeding in the sales area, as he sees his success in his work activity. If he is busy, he must be successful; his coworkers and superiors only see success in the results. He will never achieve the success and respect he wants because he does not open himself up, make himself vulnerable, risk failure, and build relationships. By isolating himself, he will not achieve his goals.

You can do the same thing with your goals. You can lie to yourself that you are doing the best you can and are on track to reach your goals. You might sabotage your progress by focusing on activities rather than results and trying to do everything yourself.

I know someone else who purposefully isolated himself. His work product was considered high quality, but he believed that he worked in a toxic environment. There was some negativity, but it was not as bad as he made it out to be. He kept withdrawing from the organization, not participating in company events, not adding his signature for the company holiday card, and other petty protests. It got to the point that the only thing that allowed him to keep his job was his work quality.

They ranked his work quality just above the pain he caused. He isolated himself until he became the poison that he was seeing around him. He ruined the relationships he had in the company and damaged his reputation. If he really believed it was an unhealthy environment and took action, he would have preserved his relationships and reputation. By isolating himself, building resentments, and relying only on his work quality, he damaged himself and reduced his options to achieve his goals.

The situation does not have to be as extreme as the one above to cause you an issue. I worked for a company with several principals. As the company evolved, I worked for different principals at different times. I had good relationships with everyone and still do today even though I no longer work there.

Toward the end of my tenure, the principal I reported to and I started to disagree. I was unsuccessful in deescalating the situation. Our disagreement came to a head, and I recommended initiating an exit plan for me as I believed the rift between us could not be closed. If I were to have stayed, I would have poisoned my relationships with people I had worked with for years.

By exiting gracefully, I was able to preserve my relationship with everyone and find a better job. By maintaining my relationships, I benefitted when an employer quizzed one of the principals for two hours about my performance. The principal gave me a stellar recommendation. Had I isolated myself without addressing the issue head-on, I would have worked in a stressful environment, poisoned my relationships, and damaged my reputation.

With downsizing and technological advances and the COVID pandemic, the opportunity to work from home has increased. Many have embraced and celebrated this opportunity to do new things. Working from home, you may complete your work in less than 40 hours, giving you time to work on your personal goals. There are benefits and drawbacks to working from home. You need to know what your goals are before you consider this option.

If you are looking to grow with your company working from home can negatively impact your growth opportunities. Eighty percent of success is showing up. If you are not in the office, you miss opportunities. Over my career, I have worked from home, and I have had people reporting to me that work from home.

The first time I worked from home was before video conferencing and other collaboration technology. I felt isolated. It was hard to maintain the relationships needed to get my job done. When the company let my boss go, I found myself adrift. It was tough to build new relationships with managers considering I was not in the office.

As a boss, I have had people work from home. It can be a successful relationship, but there are complications. When you work from home and don't or take "too long" to answer the phone, your coworkers think you are doing laundry. There is also the idea that working from home is easier and has less work. There is undoubtedly a stigma to working from home.

Even as a business owner, working from home gives the perception that you not as successful as a person who has an office. You can overcome the stigma of not having an office, but there is a cost to working from home.

There are reasons to work from home, and many people are successfully doing it. It would help if you positioned yourself to mitigate the stigma.

1. Be visible. Send emails and respond quickly. When possible, have video calls to show you are not sitting at home in your pajamas.
2. Exceed your job goals. Show that you are working effectively from home.
3. Proactively build a strong relationship with your boss and your boss's peers. You need to be visible and recognized as an asset.

There is comfort in the camaraderie of coworkers when you have a challenging job. If you are at home stewing in your own juices, it can be stressful, and you can feel singled out. The isolation can make you feel defensive and that the team is not supporting you. Feeling bitter can reflect in your work quality and your relationships. It becomes a cycle, and you can find yourself feeling more and more isolated.

You can be successful working from home. It just takes more effort to make sure you don't get isolated. Make an effort to connect with your boss and coworkers. Exceed your work goals and stay positive.

If you can manage to work from home successfully, you can achieve your other goals as well. The flexibility of working from home gives you a certain freedom to work on your side business. Not having a daily commute can provide hours of extra time each week to work on other things.

Working from home is an option that comes with pros and cons. You need to see if working from home fits your goals and then manage it to mitigate the problems. Again, the solution is to take action and put in the effort needed to maintain your performance and relationships.

Some human resource policies and general attitudes can discourage people from working together. It is funny, as, with so much talk of diversity and teamwork, many policies push us apart rather than bring us together. Executives can be afraid of showing favoritism or having the appearance of inappropriate relationships. Some will label teams as clique-ish or unfriendly when they are strong and work together.

In a corporate environment, you need to follow the rules, but you also need to build relationships with people who can help you achieve your goals, and in turn, you can help them achieve theirs. If you cannot reciprocate, you are dependent. Suppose the only return they get is the satisfaction of helping you; they will limit their help because they need to spend time working toward their goals, not focussing on helping you achieve yours. If you have a reciprocal relationship where you help each other, your relationship will be more sustainable and ultimately more satisfying.

As you build a diverse team, you need to make sure that you avoid the appearance of impropriety. Avoiding negative impressions comes into effect when you are mentoring or coaching younger people of the opposite sex. You need to ensure that your relationship never has the appearance of anything romantic. Many will avoid these relationships, but avoiding potentially productive relationships hurts you and the prospective protégé as well as your company. If you take certain precautions, you will avoid any appearance of impropriety.

The appearance of favoritism is another risk. Often the claim of favoritism stems from poor performers complaining about their better-performing colleagues. Still, there are times when people favor others because of personal reasons rather than business reasons. Favoritism is more prevalent in corporate environments, as smaller businesses tend to have more cohesive teams.

Be selective when building relationships, as this process requires effort. You only have so much time, so don't waste it on negative people who will just drain your energy rather than helping you. Some don't want you and your team to succeed; they want you to work without rocking the boat to keep them in their comfort zone. I once worked in an environment that was a little toxic because of communication issues, but it was generally a good workplace. There were two clear groups within this environment. One area was just rowing the boat. They came in, they worked, and they went home. The other area was very results-oriented. They got the deal done, or they were in trouble. The company treated people who could get the deals done differently than those who just rowed the boat. One guy just didn't understand why he wasn't getting ahead.

Our hero was a boat rower who was jealous of the deal makers. The company needed more deal makers and always encouraged people to build themselves up and grow into the jobs. The deal makers' manager took an interest in our hero and tried to guide him into the deal-making role. Sadly, he could not open his mind and learn the job. He perceived that the deal makers had it easy and didn't have to jump through the hoops like the boat rowers. He claimed favoritism when he was just unwilling to step out of his comfort zone. He wanted to continue rowing the boat while receiving the benefits of a deal maker.

After failing as a deal maker, he got more and more bitter, to the point, no one wanted to work with him at any level because dealing with him was painful. He complained about the toxic environment without ever realizing that he was a significant source of the toxicity.

The lesson to be learned is two-fold.

1. If you relate to our hero, you need to open your mind and learn the skills required to achieve your goals.
2. If you have a person like this on your team, you need to see if the value he adds outweighs the pain he causes. If there is more pain than gain, you may need to make a tough decision.

Success comes from healthy, diverse (diverse in thought as well as culture), motivated teams. It is beneficial to foster relationships with those on your team to help you achieve your goals while helping them achieve theirs.

Isolation is not just a physical phenomenon. You can be isolated in the middle of a crowded office. Office designers try to make offices more open, allowing for collaboration, but the floor plan is not the key to collaboration; it is the team, the people, that make collaboration happen. If you stick a bunch of individuals in an open office space and do no team building, you still have a group of individuals, not a team. You can have a team spread across the country that is much stronger than a team in a small office. You need to consider your work environment and what you can do to be a strong team member while gathering people around you to work with you.

It is nearly impossible to build a strong team with people who are working just to have a job. You will have even more trouble achieving your goals if YOU are there for just a paycheck.

Suppose you are not a manager with authority to hire and fire people; how do you build a team? You need to find people in the company that you work well with and collaborate with them. That is a difficult task, as you may need to build relationships and reach out to people outside of your typical work environment. Do you see a pattern? Building relationships is not possible if you isolate yourself or immerse yourself solely within your work environment.

Your physical work environment has an impact on your ability to collaborate. We have heard people rail against offices—managers with "closed door" policies. Walls and doors were frowned upon, so they developed the open office. The intention was to bring people together, to collaborate, and help people work in teams. The open concept has had some unintended consequences. The noise and lack of privacy have lead people to develop strategies to isolate themselves in a crowd. To function, they give themselves the illusion of privacy, trying to block out noise.

One way they do this is by listening to music at their desks. You walk through offices, and you see people with their heads down wearing earbuds, adding music to dull their situational awareness and help them focus on their tasks. Many use other strategies, like hijacking conference rooms for telephone calls.

The open concept pushes people to take action to isolate themselves. Having worked in an open office environment, I understand why people do this, as it can be hard to focus through the noise. When the office initially had a closed office culture, this problem is compounded when the workers are thrust into an open environment. Collaboration does not just happen without a collaborative team. When multi-discipline teams working toward a common objective are all put together in their own space, they can work effectively. I have seen the open office work.

This section aims to recognize your working environment and how you can work in it effectively without isolating yourself.

You can't always choose your colleagues, and it can be tough to build a strong team with people who are just at work for a job. Most people are just glad to have a job, or that is what they tell themselves and others. It is human nature to want to achieve; some may not know how to do it or may not want to put in the effort to accomplish it. They go to work, put in their time, and go home.

To achieve big goals, people need to go beyond the minimum effort required. To achieve your goals, you need to put everything into it. You need to sacrifice and work hard.

- To lose weight, you need to give up excess calorie intake and increase working out.
- Writing this book, I gave up excess sleep and wrote every morning.
- If you want to get ahead at work, you need to step out of your comfort zone and push yourself beyond the minimum work effort.

Throughout a good portion of my career, I headed teams. I would constantly strive to get my people promoted out of my team. That might seem like I worked against my best interests, but I found it to be the opposite and very effective. As mentioned before, it is nearly impossible to build a strong team of people there just for a job. By showing people that I wanted to see them succeed, my team was an escalator up. I set exceptionally high expectations, and my people needed to work. I exposed them to people who could help them advance and made sure to talk them up. We were a team. They completed their work with excellence so that I could achieve my goals. I showcased them and let them achieve their goals. This process built not only team members but friends that I have had for years.

You can motivate people who are there for just a job to embrace achievement. When they see they can achieve goals, they will work harder to achieve them. As a junior team leader, management gave me mediocre-performing teams and expected me to bring them up to speed. By showing the benefits of performance, many were motivated to step up and achieve goals.

I worked in a group where the head was not a team builder; he was a control freak. Because he wanted control of everything, he seemed to attract people who wanted to be told what to do and do their job, but nothing else. Within his open floor environment, everyone used earbuds and looked at their screens. They all worked but did not achieve. The manager built a culture that attracted drones.

From the outside, this looked great. A group of people; getting the job done. When you pull back the cover, you find something else. Now you encounter a group of people who are not satisfied with their work and lack the ambition to find something better. How do you build a team with people like that? It is not easy.

I knew that developing my team within that environment; I could not expect excellent work. This situation could make an interesting case study. I had to set up the group to achieve my results without pushing people beyond their capabilities. I brought in training programs, set up a productivity program, and built targets to get people to focus on achievement. Despite this effort, I could not overcome the groups' inertia of putting in the minimum.

I understand why I wasn't successful. Senior management continued to reinforce the "I tell you what to do, and you do it" culture. They wanted to build a scalable workforce but could not give up control. I concluded that to succeed, I needed to adapt to the environment.

You can succeed in toxic and micromanaged environments. Thriving in those environments requires you to have a sharper focus on your goals. You can't expect support from your leaders, so you need to have an environment-specific strategy and adjust your tactics to overcome the environment's challenges. Your success is your responsibility. You may have disadvantages, your environment might be hostile, but you have the power to succeed.

Team building is another opportunity to use the OODA loop.

Suppose your target is to build a solid team. You have the strategy to develop the people into strong team members. What are you going to do?

Observe – you see that the team has not had leadership

Orient – You see that the people need direction and goals

Decide – You put together a plan to support and train the team

<u>Act</u> – Execute the leadership and training plan.

Never lose sight of the objective of building these relationships. You have goals you want to achieve. To achieve these goals, you need a successful team, and first, you need to develop a team. Because you need this team to support your goal, ensure that the goal is interesting to them. Are your goals interesting to you, and can you make them attractive to others? Sometimes, you can get people to help you as a favor, which they will do because they like you. Relying on the kindness of others will work occasionally, but the better strategy is to get people to help you because they share an interest in your project.

A great way to prepare yourself for achieving your goals and getting others interested is to socialize your idea. You need to be open to feedback and comfortable with the audience. When your idea is in its infancy, you need to keep it within your inner circle. Napoleon Hill called this inner circle his mastermind group. This group contains your most valuable advisors, who will encourage and caution you based on facts. They want you to succeed and have the experience to give you relevant feedback. Once the idea has made it through the mastermind vetting, it is time to socialize it more broadly to see who would be interested in working with you.

Previously I attended a course on starting a business. A marketing professional ran the course and highlighted the value of socializing ideas and understanding your customer and target market. Many of the exercises were to talk about our business ideas; socializing these with like-minded people and experts. The trainer and other experts gave feedback on the business ideas. By socializing our ideas, we were able to get feedback that made our goals more achievable. Reflecting on an earlier chapter, this was an opportunity to live "Shark Tank" rather than just watching. Watch the show for inspiration; go out and live it to achieve your goals.

The one caveat to socializing the idea is understanding that it is not a committee decision. Just because someone suggests a change does not mean you have to comply. Remember, this is not a formal process. You need to take the information you gather and make a decision on how you want to proceed. If you have a great idea but don't have your groups well defined, don't hold back. Build your groups and ideas at the same time. Toastmasters provides an example of why you should be cautious feedback from your outer circle. Toastmasters help people build public speaking skills, sponsor speaking competitions from the club level, and escalate to the international level.

When members win at the club level, they get to speak in front of other chapters to get feedback from new sources. They gather so much information, as everyone, from beginners to experts, has an opinion on delivery. Finally, it comes down to the competitor on stage. It is their speech; they need to deliver it. Based on the feedback, the competitor needs to decide what to accept and what to reject. A coach or mentor with expertise can guide the speaker on which advice to take. You don't want to change your speech and potentially make it less likely to win.

When setting goals, experts tell us to make them clear. By clear, they mean SMART: Specific, Measurable, Achievable, Relevant, and Time-bound. That is important. Having SMART goals provides a structure making them easier to achieve. To reach your full potential, you need to use all available tools to achieve your goals. These tools include getting help from your teams. What can you do to get more people to help you? You need to go beyond SMART goals. Your goals should be exciting, not only to you but also to other people.

For example, you can make writing a book a SMART goal.

Specific: I will write the first draft of a book on team building

Measurable: I will write every day.

Achievable: I have allocated the time and have the knowledge

Relevant: I want to write the book

Time-bound: I will do it in 90-days

That is a SMART goal. Are you excited about it? Can you make other people excited about it? Being excited about it gives you a better chance of achieving it. If the people around you are excited about it, they will help motivate you to achieve it.

More questions to ask yourself, using the book-writing goal. Why do you want to write a book? Credibility? Earn Money? Sell companion products?

As I write, I sometimes feel discouraged. There are days when I lack the inspiration I need. I feel insecure about my abilities. It's at these low points that the reasons behind the goal are essential. You then remind yourself WHY you are doing this.

The Reasons Why:

Message - I have a message that I want to share and feel confident that people need to hear.

Opportunities for speaking engagements – I enjoy public speaking. Having a published book opens more doors.

Book Sales – I want to be a successful author, so I will continue to write until I achieve that goal.

Those are the reasons to excite me. How do I excite the people around me?

I have socialized and given presentations on parts of my book, which has generated other people's interest. I have demonstrated how they can benefit, and they feel like they are part of the project. Sometimes I think my team is more excited about my goals than I am; it helps keep me on track. Whether you are a team leader or member, you can use this technique to make your team stronger.

As you grow and your goals get bigger, you will start delegating tasks. With the book, I delegated editing and other tasks. Delegating to subordinates makes me a team leader, taking my role beyond team membership. It is best to separate yourself from your subordinates to lead and show results by relying on the team you lead. Because your results depend on others, you need to hold them accountable and be willing to take action when they do not perform. The first place you will probably experience this is in the workplace or as a volunteer leader. You can adapt those skills learned through these experiences, using them when delegating tasks to your team, rather than your individual efforts.

Getting your team to produce at a high level is exponentially more challenging than relying only on your own work. The benefit of leading a capable team is scaling your efforts. Your team members may not be able to mirror your efforts, but in a team of five who can each perform at 80% of your level, your team can produce 400% of your individual performance. That is the power of a team.

Let's recap and expand on the idea of a team from the introduction of this book.

The ideal team will have:

Sponsors – These are the people who pull you up. They can be bosses or other leaders that want to help you grow.

I attracted sponsors to my book project by asking them to write endorsements for the cover. I only approached those that I knew, many of whom I worked with before. Later, I learned that I should stretch and use my book project to find new sponsors for my network.

The number one sponsor relationship will be an employer. It can be your direct boss, a company executive outside of your reporting line, an entrepreneur, or a key customer. To be noticed by these potential sponsors, you need to be interesting. Can you offer them value? Are you are a high-performing employee, providing the company and the sponsor value? If you are a high performer, this value can carry beyond the term of your employment. Those sponsors may be willing to help you even when your company connection closes.

I have built a reputation for achieving results and helping people in my network. My sponsors show great interest in me because there is a good possibility that I will reciprocate in the future.

Coaches/Mentors – To differential, you would pay your coaches and not your mentors. Mentors are people that offer you advice with whom you have a personal relationship. I have several mentors, and I am sure you do too; perhaps you don't think of them in such a formal way.

Becoming a published author is an exciting project. My coach and mentors were all excited and very supportive of my project. Mentors are so important that I have dedicated a section to them. Essential parts of building these relationships are networking. It is up to you to find the mentor and vet and evaluate them to ensure they are qualified and compatible. There are many touting themselves as coaches, even though unqualified. Because a relationship is vital, you must ensure that your personalities are compatible, or you will not get enough value from the relationship.

Peers – These are the people around you, your coworkers, associates, friends, and others you surround yourself with. Remember that it is hard to soar with the eagles when you surround yourself with turkeys.

When developing my team, I found my peers were a mixed bag. Some were very excited, some couldn't care less, and a few were almost hostile. In navigating this group, I made mistakes by spending time convincing people on the fence rather than supporting my supporters. I learned a lot from the TED Talk by Derek Sivers – How to start a movement. As peers, we need to learn to support each other. Not all of your peers will have equal standing on your team, as some will be in your inner circle of supportive peers and others in your outer circle. The outer circle can add value but may discourage you, so you shouldn't share all of your ideas and aspirations with your outer circle.

Subordinates – These are not just people who work for you. These are people you are helping to grow; you are their sponsor or mentor. In return, they do things for you. I often use my kids to do tasks that free me up to do more important things, and in return, I give them guidance and support.

I was able to mobilize people to help me with my goals in exchange for assisting their growth. As their sponsor or mentor,

I was able to get them excited about helping me. Choose intelligent, hard-working, and self-reliant subordinates, as you don't want to chase them to get work done.

Many people shun delegation because it is easier to do it themselves. The process of working yourself is more comfortable than building a team. However, the scale provided by the team makes achieving the goal more effortless. You are limited by time and energy when you rely only on yourself.

As a management team member, I push to get my strategy accepted by the other team members. I rely on my performance to build credibility and show others how to use my process to help them achieve their goals. To be a successful leadership team member, I need to influence the other members and help them achieve their goals. When you are a change agent, your presence changes those around you.

Notice I called this your team, not your service providers. Except for the coach, these are not people you pay. It would be best to build relationships with these people as they have no compulsion to help you. Demonstrate a sincere attitude of giving, and know that you will give much more than you receive. In this process, you will find that other people will be more willing to help you by seeing you help others.

You need to make your goals exciting to them to attract them to your cause. I used this when publishing my first book.

As you influence other people, other people influence you. You tend to reflect the characteristics of those with whom you associate. We joke about pet owners starting to look like their pets. We begin to act like the people surrounding us. You need to be sure that you don't start taking the attributes of those you are not trying to emulate.

"You are the average of the five people you spend the most time with."

— JIM ROHN

Reflection

Who is on your team? Do you have the people you need to achieve your goals?

Catalog your relationships in your journal. Who can help you achieve your goals, and what can you do for them?

Who do you need to build a relationship with to complete your team?

Does your work environment help you or hurt you? How do you need to change or adapt to your environment to execute your plan effectively?

You will not always be able to meet in person. How will you utilize tools like video conferencing and collaboration technology to build your team?

Takeaways

Working through teams is more challenging than working on your own, but the rewards from leveraging your team can be so large that your performance can improve exponentially.

Like any sports team, you need specific types of team members to ensure a capable and functional team. If you only have subordinates, you will have no one to pull you up. If you only have sponsors, you won't scale your efforts and do all the work yourself.

If your job is not supportive of your goals, you need to work on these separately. Separate goals mean building a different team and developing new relationships. It is ideal to have your work and personal goals aligned, but this is not always achievable. You are responsible for building your teams to achieve your goals.

This description of your team is a 360-degree view of the people around you. You can't divide the team into equal quadrants, as you will have fewer sponsors and mentors than peers and subordinates. Also, you will have many more opportunities to mentor than being mentored. As you get known as a qualified mentor, people will seek you out just as you seek others. As your team develops and gains strength, you will attract people toward you. Even those who don't have a plan inherently know that relationships with high-performing people can benefit them.

Life is a team sport. Everyone can be more successful by helping each other out. Not everyone is worthy of your help. Some will take your experience and use it to push others aside. Others do not want to leave their comfort zone and are not coachable. You will learn to differential between those who are not worthy and those who are not.

You might consider your team weak. Not to worry, we will be talking about building and strengthening your teams later in the book!

Results

There is an African word "Ubuntu" which translates to "I am , because we are". You will achieve more with an effective team. With a strong team, you can multiply your efforts.

You benefit at all levels.

- Leveraging personal interaction builds strong relationships
- Building multiple strong relationships makes strong teams
- Strong teams multiply your efforts giving you better results

You will be able to develop ideas into results. As your team develops, you will have levels of sub-teams that will help you grow. For example:

1. Inner Circle – Your most trusted advisors, help you hone your ideas
2. Outer Circle – Your primary team that helps you socialize your ideas and execute your plans
3. Greater Network – Your acquaintances that support your objectives and increase your results

Once you build your team, you will achieve more than you could ever have done on your own!

NOTES

NOTES

NOTES

CHAPTER 7
Social Media, The New Normal

Social Media impacted our lives. You expose yourself to distractions and negative impacts if you use social media, but avoiding it almost guarantees you being left behind. Social media is an essential tool for relationship building, but it can hurt your relationships if used poorly. I think it is so important that I am dedicating an entire chapter to this topic.

Technology intended to bring people together but has had the opposite effect and has left many people more isolated. Video conferences and social media gives you access to people all over the world. I recently gave a presentation to a group in Great Britain that was made possible through technology. How can I say that technology is holding you back? Technology does have the potential to open the door to the world if used correctly. It also has the negative potential to build walls that keeps you from achieving your full potential.

Technology allows you to spend more time away from people. You fool yourself that you are networking when you are merely connecting with people on social media. Why do we do this? There is a low chance of rejection, and you get instant gratification. Social media, by design, makes you feel good. I have contacts all over the world; this does not mean that I have a worldwide network. I have never spoken to these people, so I have no relationship with them.

I do not send out connection requests to people I don't know, but I accept requests from people I don't know if their background shows that knowing them might be helpful. I have built relationships and done business with people I've met on social media. To get to that point, I needed to reach out and make an effort to build the relationship. I had to take a risk and open myself up to rejection.

Experiencing rejection can make you act like the wounded bear and retreat to your cave. You take the easy path and focus on non-relationship tasks. Avoiding relationship building is unsatisfying and puts you at a disadvantage. If you are going to succeed, you need to make connections.

Social media increased both the isolation and influence, even though it was supposed to bring us together and express ourselves.

Most of us use social media to keep up with friends, family, or professional contacts. Social media is beneficial for keeping track of loved ones who live far away and interacting with friends we haven't seen in a while. It is also an outlet to network with people you may not have the opportunity to see in person.

Social media lets us observe activities and interact with people we don't visit because we are too busy or too far away. The challenge becomes that your interaction is typically very generic or impersonal. These interactions are generally public, and others can see and interject into your conversations. Because of the observable nature of social media, you don't have the intimate conversations on which you build relationships.

I received a private message through social media site from a former coworker wanting to schedule a time to talk. I must admit that having someone ask me for a call did feel funny. I was swamped, but I made some time, and once we were on the phone, we had a great conversation. We talked about the projects we were working on and set up a time for future contact to collaborate on projects.

Social media is a great tool, but you can't stop there. If you only interact via social media, you will not get to the deeper levels you need to build friendships and business relationships, which only come with personal interaction. Continue using social media, but make the time to reach out and build the relationships you need to gain the connections you need to be happy and successful. You can have thousands of "friends" and "contacts" on social media, but you will be isolating yourself without personal connections, and you will be lonely.

Social media is also touted as a place for expressing yourself. You are supposed to be creative and open to express your feelings and art; however, we found that the critics reign. When people do express themselves, they are crushed by critics. It has gotten to the point where this extreme criticism has been categorized as a type of bullying, cyber-bullying.

Many do not want to hear about your success and do not want you to show that you are working toward a clear objective. Through your actions, you indicate that it is possible to work and succeed. Those who blame others for their failures can lash out at the post because they sense that the most significant cause of their problems lies within themselves. They get angry, and here you find that they do not have your best interest at heart. They bring equilibrium to their lives by trying to diminish you.

Criticism is easy to accomplish online. People have the power to confront without the limitations brought by personal contact. Let's picture social media as a family at the dinner table.

- Someone mentions their faith. Do you call them a clown and ridicule their faith?
- Someone talks about losing weight. Do you tell the person they'll never lose weight?
- Someone wants to start a project, take a class for self-improvement. Do you mock the person?

If I were to guess, I would say that you would not. You would be more supportive, even if you feel differently. Generally, people keep a more civilized tone in person. Being able to criticize others while hiding behind a computer screen can be satisfying to some people, so be mindful about what you share online.

If you are excited about a project and post it online, the critics can start the influence campaign to stop you, keeping you at their level. People influence you daily. It is best to limit the negative influences. You can do this by not exposing yourself to nameless online critics. If you want feedback, you need to find people with expertise and your best interests at heart. We'll cover this later in the book.

Social media gives the illusion of a relationship. You have interactions that seem like conversations. You read comments and see pictures that give the appearance of connecting. This interaction is not a reliable connection, just surface noise. Content posted online tends to be filled with hyperbole and skewed to the positive side of life.

Close relationships are built on communication and getting to know people, the good, the bad, and the ugly. Think about times that you have spilled your guts on a lousy circumstance in your life. To whom did you speak? It was probably someone close to you. Someone you know and trust. It is not something you would discuss with someone who is not close to you.

I have a significant obstacle to relationship building, and when I read Brene Brown's Daring Greatly, I found that many men share this problem. I don't feel comfortable sharing my weaknesses and don't want to appear vulnerable. It is easier to be 'strong' and not share. Brené Brown describes how society gives men mixed messages, saying they should be more vulnerable, but reactions to men being vulnerable give the opposite message.

This resistance to vulnerability seems to permeate society for both sexes and can drive people into isolation and impede the building of relationships. Social media exacerbates the resistance to vulnerability through exaggerated posts and negative feedback.

The progression of this isolation starts with your reluctance to be vulnerable.

- We have problems, and we don't want to open ourselves up to discuss with others.
- We build our relationships primarily online.

- We see our online 'friends' achieving great things and having fun without understanding the cost or if the achievements are real.
- We wallow in our problems and start resenting others' success.
- We wonder why we have these problems while everyone else is doing well.

We forget that most social media posts emphasize or even exaggerate only the positive parts of people's lives. People tend to portray themselves in the best light online. Even when complaining, they are showcasing themselves and merely looking for positive reinforcement. They only post the parts of their lives they want the public to see, so they tend to exaggerate. Look at your posts. Do you offer only the positive side of the story? Do you exaggerate? If you are exaggerating, do you think everyone else is showing their complete story? They aren't. Social media is not designed that way.

Building a relationship exclusively on social media is an artificial relationship, nothing more than posturing without sharing. I am talking about relationships based primarily online with no deeper or personal interaction. If you have developed a relationship with someone through conversation and shared experiences and keep in touch via social media, that is not an artificial relationship.

Examples for me are people from high school that were not close friends, and I have not had social interaction with them for decades. With half a lifetime of twists and turns, I know nothing about them other than what they post online. They are acquaintances, not close friends.

A little while back, I met with some of them at a get-together. When we spoke and rekindled the relationships, it demonstrated how empty the online connection truly was. But the point I need to make is to highlight how real the online relationship can seem. Suppose we base a majority of our social life on social media; we then tend to compare our real lives to our peer's posts that only show the parts of their lives they want us to see. We don't have an outlet to discuss the posts, so we don't understand that other people have similar issues, making us feel alone and isolated. This isolation can make us feel like we are in a rowboat on the ocean, surrounded by water with nothing to drink, keeping us focused on our problems and not on our goals.

Social media is a great way to keep in touch with friends and family. We get to share the pieces of our lives we want to showcase. We can share jokes, have fun, go overboard with political discourse, or seek the information we need. It is an excellent tool if we maintain the perspective that it is not a replacement for one on one personal interaction.

I have been pushing myself to make time to get together with people. It is incredible how hard it can be to schedule. I find that meeting for breakfast or coffee works well as you spend 45 minutes talking, which adds so much more value than hours online. Phone calls work, but video meeting availability brings people from all over the world to you and seeing people's facial expressions adds to the conversation. You can respond not just to the words but to the facial expressions.

Relationships take work. Social media gives the illusion of an easy way to build relationships. Still, you end up isolated even when "surrounded by 4,500 of your closest friends and family". You are in the rowboat on the ocean, looking for something to drink. You need to move beyond it.

Social media can distract you from your goals. You can get bored with what you are doing and need to take a "little break" that turns into hours of wasted time. We all need downtime. We need to decompress and recharge. A distraction is not downtime; it is a waste of valuable time, that could be better allocated to actual downtime If your mind started to wander in the days before social media, you would go for a walk and get back to work. We now have a stream of memes (pictures with comic messages), videos, and other instant entertainment that takes you farther from your work than taking some deep breaths or going for a walk does. The distraction caused by instant entertainment takes you longer to get back to action. I mentioned earlier that I once fell into this trap. I like to watch old comedy videos online. I would take a break and start watching Rodney Dangerfield or Richard Pryor, and my ten-minute break would suddenly last two hours. There is so much entertainment content that it is easy to get lost.

Next comes the distraction of the siren call of our cell phone. We get notifications for everything. It seems that cell phones are for everything but phone calls. Text message – buzz-buzz; Facebook post – buzz-buzz, new YouTube video buzz-buzz. We are inundated with notifications.

The simplistic answer is just to turn your phone off, but that doesn't work. I'll use myself as an example. During the day, My company expects that I monitor and respond to many things on my phone. I work in an open office, so I keep my phone on vibrate. It is hard to differentiate between the urgent and the meaningless.

Should my boss text me, and I need to respond. Therefore, when I hear the buzz-buzz, I respond. There is social media messaging that I need to keep on top of because of things I post, and I need to respond in a relatively timely way. If I hear the buzz buzz, and I see that I need to respond to a potential customer, I can finish my task, but I need to respond soon after that.

My company just installed a video instant messenger on our network. It is unclear if and when we are permitted to ignore these. I can be in the middle of an important task that requires concentration. I am in the zone and then "ding dong." I have someone waiting on my computer screen.

We need to manage and balance these things. When I am writing and working on a piece that takes a lot of thought and concentration, I will leave my technology alone and bring a notebook into a private space. I try to work at times when other people aren't. As I am writing this chapter, it is around six in the morning. My phone has buzzed a couple of times, but since no one can expect me to respond at this time, I am ignoring it.

Another online distraction is empire-building games. These games give constant achievements, and you get penalties for not paying enough attention. Many years ago, I was fascinated by "Mafia Wars." It was a game where you built your empire, and you got more power by attacking and winning fights against other players.

If you were not there to fight back, especially if your opponent had more assets than you, you could lose a lot of power. I found that people were attacking me while I was at work. It led me to start checking the game during the workday. It did not have any material impact on my job, but there could have been better uses for my time.

If I could do my job and build my artificial empire, why couldn't I create a real one? I could have been writing my tenth book now rather than my second. I could have done charity work. I could have gotten a part-time job, but my online empire had me hooked.

There are so many empire-building games that draw you in and encourage you to play; instead, why don't you focus on building your real empire? These games feed on our desire to win. We all want to grow. We want people's respect, and we want to be the boss. We want people to like and love us.

It is hard to reach that level of excitement and achievement in the real world. We have flat org charts, meaning fewer supervisory roles, so there is less growth potential. It is hard to build that empire. We have created a criticism culture, so people tear each other down rather than build each other up. People gather at the bottom and pull others down.

We know somewhere in our minds that it is wrong to race to the bottom, so we look for opportunities to win. These online games that we can now carry on our phones give the illusion of real-life winning. While commuting to work or in a boring meeting, we find an easy path to feel like we are winning and put our energy into that at the expense of real success.

My most extreme example of online distraction was from a news story out of Asia. A man living with his parents lost his job. While he was looking for another job, he started playing an online empire-building game. He became obsessed, and he put all his energy into the game and no longer had time to look for a job.

His parents pushed him and urged move on with his life, but his life was his game. The parents then took extreme measures and hired people who played the same game to attack and destroy their son's online empire. They destroyed his empire, and he went out and got a job.

The above example is extreme, but it demonstrates how we can get so involved in these distractions at the expense of our success. It is easy to feel like we are losing in life. In today's society, we have gaps in our lives:

- We feel isolated.
- It is harder to find career success.
- It is harder to build relationships.
- We ignore our spiritual needs.
- We carry more debt.
- We are more out of shape.
- We don't address depression, anxiety, and other issues.

In our fast-paced lives, we look for escapes. Escapes like drugs, alcohol, or pornography are no easy to carry to the workplace, but empire games can go anywhere, and since they are not an extreme vice, we feel okay with them. I do not believe that playing games are as self-destructive as substance abuse or sex addictions. However, they can weave into your life in a way that distracts you from what you want to achieve, giving you a false sense of achievement and temporary satisfaction. Game satisfaction is so fleeting that you need to strive for the next level to keep the flow going.

Those who don't play games may be asking why we are discussing this issue. Games are not only for young people. I know players 50+ with good jobs who play these games and get immersed in them. Some even have special gaming rooms in their houses, like others have gyms.

It is okay to have a hobby and to play games. I practice martial arts, and I read. I don't spend 100% of my time striving for my goals. We need to ensure that our hobbies are healthy and do not detract from our quest for success.

If you are reading this book, there is a good chance that you are not satisfied with your current situation. You need to make some decisions. Is your online life helping you or hindering you?

You can use all social media for networking. I will focus on LinkedIn since it is a professional social media platform. Social media can communicate a detailed picture of you and your brand, and people will judge you by what they see on your social media profiles. Knowing you will be judged, it is prudent to be cognizant of how you portray yourself on social media.

When you are using social media to network, you are showcasing your brand. You are showing why you as a product should be interesting to other people. This is not an online trophy case to display your greatness. You want others to see you as a resource, not a narcissist. Before developing your online presence, carefully consider the audience you want to attract. Some pages can best be compared to a little kid trying to get his mom's attention yelling, " Mom, Mom, Mom, look what I did. Look, Look, Look." Don't get me wrong. I have my career information and my accomplishments on my LinkedIn Profile. I put content on my page that would be interesting to the people I want as prospects.

If people are looking at your page, they have taken an interest in you. You don't want to ruin it by appearing narcissistic. If your pages portray you as self-centered (loaded only with selfies and personal accomplishments), you will turn off your prospect. If you have articles and videos that of interest to your prospect along with the information about yourself, they will stay interested in you. If you have personal and prospect-centric content, they will feel like they already know you before meeting in person. If done well, your social media can ease your entrance into a networking relationship.

If you were to look at my LinkedIn profile, you would see:

- A video I put together on communication styles
- An invitation to one of my book signings
- An article on housing
- An advertisement for a seminar I will be hosting
- A thank you to a group I spoke to by invitation.
- A link to a TED talk that I found interesting

The posts are a balance of interesting content and self-promotion. It showcases me, but it has content that like-minded people find stimulating. They view my content because it relates to them. Even my self-centric content is about other people— seminars to help other people, presentations to explain the book, and a thank you for your invitation. I am projecting myself as the secondary character to my prospect's main character. To attract other people to you, you want to be interesting; it makes it easier to network. Being boring puts an obstacle in your path before you even start. To overcome that obstacle, you have to work to convince people you are not as dull as your LinkedIn shows before you can even start the conversation.

Reflection

Journal time! How are you using social media? Is social media helping or hindering you in your relationship building?

How healthy are your relationships? Do you have in-depth conversations with others, or do you dabble at the surface?

For one week, keep a "distractions log," writing down what you do with your time. How often and for how long are you using social media and other media to distract yourself?

Takeaways

Social media can be a tool and a distraction. Using social media with intention will help you maintain relationships and gain potential introductions to new people.

You want to read books, write a blog or exercise, but find you have no time and don't understand why. You will be surprised at how much idle time you have. You will probably find that distractions you think are taking minutes are taking hours. We limit our kids' access to computers and television. Shouldn't we do the same for ourselves?

Your goals are not going to achieve themselves, and you need to work at them. If you anticipate that your goal will take 60 hours to accomplish, spending ten hours a week, you can accomplish it in six weeks. But consider doing it in three weeks by working on it for twenty hours a week. You might be asking, "where can I find the time?" Your Distractions Log will show you where you can find the time.

Results

You are building and maintaining relationships with a combination of social media and traditional contact. You have an inner circle that is privy to your vulnerability and a larger or outer circle that can help you achieve your goals.

You are building these relationships to foster cultivated friendships. You help your friends when they need it, and they help you.

You are succeeding together, and you build strong relationships.

NOTES

NOTES

NOTES

PART 4

MENTORS

CHAPTER 8
Finding Your Mentors

There has been a secular shift in our society, a breakdown in organized activity and supportive relationships. We have seen a membership decline in volunteer and religious organizations. These organizations have historically been the basis of learning to work together and learning from one another. This decline, combined with workplace culture changes, has severely damaged the mentor – protégé relationship. Isolation due to the COVID pandemic has compounded the problem.

As mentioned earlier, we are isolated and spend less one on one time than the generations before us. Technology allows you to collaborate separately or in impersonal groups. Separate collaboration sounds like an oxymoron, but it results from conference calls, outsourcing, and online communication. Technology has allowed and even encouraged us to work in isolation, often from our homes. A former colleague had half of his team in India, and the rest spread across the United States, many of which he has never met in person. Also, he worked from home in a different state from his boss. In these situations, how do you build relationships? How do you learn from one another? If you can't learn the required skills at work and no organizations outside of work offer the opportunity to learn, how do you get ahead?

Those who were able to work from home during the COVID-19 pandemic experienced this isolation and got a taste of the difficulties in developing relationships. We feel like things are happening that we can't see, and it is hard for managers to determine what tasks are being completed, if people are as productive as they should be or if people need guidance. Technology allows you to connect without being present. It is like you are on a tether doing a spacewalk, and your staff and boss are in the spaceship. You feel exposed and alone.

The solution to this shortage of guidance is going out and building relationships. You need to build relationships at work and outside of work, and this starts with networking. People get nervous when they hear the word "networking," but you probably do it now and don't realize it.

Imagine you just paid $9.00 for a Bud Light after standing in line for 20 minutes. You look across the expanse of a dingy hotel ballroom, and you see people grouped by company. Over there, against the wall, are people manically pecking at their phones. Then meandering through the crowd, you see sad-looking people desperately trying to make eye contact with people in the groups, and oh no, one has made eye contact with you. He is approaching, his smile wide and his business card extended.

This situation is how many envision networking because this is how you have experienced it in the past. You go to networking groups because "everyone is there to network." You have to ask yourself, is this effective networking? When you hear the word networking, you may think of uncomfortable sales introductions. That is the standard approach to networking. "Hi, I'm Chad. Do you need insurance, investments, work done on your house?" Even if you are in sales, selling your product to someone you met two minutes ago is not an effective networking strategy. Networking is about meeting people and building relationships.

If you meet someone you want to sell to, want to mentor or give you a job, focus on the relationship. People want to deal with people they know and trust. It is your job to be a relationship builder.

Networking is an activity and not a type of social gathering. Most people do it poorly because of misguided expectations. Networking is not about what you need; it is what you can offer others.

You may believe that you need to network to sell your products. Giving the other person what they need still works and makes you a more effective networker. Do you want to sell to people who don't need or want your product? Do you want to go to an event filled with people you don't need to meet? If you have a room full of people you want to meet, does it make sense to spend the entire time on your phone? If you are not an effective networker, these are results you can expect. How many times have you gone to a networking event and had similar results?

You can avoid ineffective networking by applying a few principles.

1. Have a goal
2. Do your homework

3. Be engaged

Networking takes effort, so you should have a goal. Even if it is just to meet new people, have a goal before you start. When I attend a conference, I first take the time to see what my company needs; looking for investment opportunities, looking for new vendors or selling assets. By having a clear purpose, I can target the people I can serve. I can find those seeking assets or looking to sell products that I need. I am looking for people I can help; by giving them what they need, I get what I need to achieve my goals.

To achieve these objectives, you need to do your homework. I like to get an attendee list before the event to research the people and companies. Knowing who will be there allows you to target prospects and avoid events that don't have any candidates that fit your criteria.

When I arrive at the event, I am there to work and focus on my objectives. I went to a conference with a colleague that cost about $2,000 each. My colleague spent most of his time on his phone, wasting the $2,000 fee paid by the company. When you attend an event, you need to be engaged and focus on the people you want to meet.

> *"You will get all you want in life by giving enough other people what they want."*
> — ZIG ZIGLAR

Networking bears fruit the same way.

Where should you start your networking? Should you go out of your way to join networking groups? My advice is to begin networking in your environment. A family gathering, church, volunteer meeting, conference, or training session for work is where you should start networking.

If you feel uncomfortable with the idea of networking where you live, remember you are building relationships. Some might turn into business or mentor relationships; you are networking, not selling. You are merely meeting people and increasing your social circle size. You will make new friends too!

So you are at a function, how do you start? The good thing about starting in a group of familiar people is that you have a common interest in initiating a conversation. At the conference I mentioned earlier, my cell phone battery was running low, so I headed to the charging station. There I found some people awkwardly staring at their cell phones. I commented on how great it was to have the charging station, which opened the conversational flood gates. People need the invitation to talk, and my simple comment opened it up. Some of these people were salespeople who you would think would start the conversation, but you can't rely on that. You need to initiate it.

You have opened the conversation. What now? Have you ever had someone dominate your time talking about themselves? How did you feel? I was at a legal meeting and had to spend several hours with our attorney. He spent that time regaling me with his greatness, talking about all the great things he did for our company and all the great things he can do. On and on and on, he went, and I had no escape; I had to grin and bear it. He was a bore, and I felt like he only saw me as a cash cow.

Don't be that guy! You want to focus on the other person. Understand your goal; is it to talk about yourself or to build relationships? If your goal is to build relationships, you need to make the other person feel important and want to talk to you.

To accomplish that, you need to focus on the subject most relevant to the person, get them to talk about themselves, and you need to listen. You can use the information they give you about themselves and inject information about yourself to guide the conversation and make it a productive relationship-building exercise

If you take a genuine interest in the other person, they will likely want to talk to you. Some people just won't click with you no matter what you do. Just let them pass. If there is nothing you can do to build the relationship, drop it, and move along. When you find the person who is open to chatting with you, focus on them. There will be plenty of time for you to talk later. You need to listen because you should ask probing questions. Listening does two things.

- It demonstrates that you are taking an interest in the other person. If you ask probing questions, you show that you are listening and interested in hearing more about them.
- You are ostensibly interviewing the person to see if they are a candidate for what you need. You will determine if they are a prospect for your product, a mentor, could give you a job, or work for you.

Once you have the information you wanted, you either want to build a relationship or don't. It is now time for a graceful exit. Always show gratitude. Thank the person for their time and say goodbye. If you think the person is a prospect, you can say something like, "Wow, thanks for your time and filling me in on XYZ. I am very and would like to continue our conversation. If you have time, let's grab a coffee in the next week or two." If they are not a prospect, still thank the person for their time and excuse yourself. If they are pushy, just say you need to go to the restroom. Almost everyone will let you go with that.

Joining networking groups can be a great resource as well, but they are a little trickier. It is good to go with another person to tag team and rescue each other when needed. Having a person you know and trust at your side can increase your confidence; you know that you have a friendly face to work with if you start to strike out. If they are in a conversation, they can invite you in, and if you each know what the other is looking for, you can introduce prospects. If you don't have a wingman, you can still be successful at these events. Everyone is there to meet other people, but most people don't know how to do it. Just like the other groups, you will need to initiate the conversation. Here it is a little more challenging, but the more you do it, the easier it gets.

You have made the first contact with a person who could be a prospect and finds you interesting enough to continue the conversation. What now? Initiate the idea of a meeting over breakfast or coffee, a 30 – 45 minute meeting. Framing the meeting's legnth will help you have a more productive conversation. You still focus on the other person, but you start to interject information about yourself into the conversation. David Miller has written several marketing books. His theory of marketing has the customer as the hero, and you are the guide. .The point is that you are a supporting character in the relationship. Your prospect is the hero of their story, and you can help guide them to success.

Once you have established the relationship, you can start integrating more of yourself into the conversation. If this is a Mentor-Protégé relationship, you will introduce more of yourself earlier since that is the point of the relationship. How the relationship proceeds from there is up to you and the other person.

Patience is paramount in building lasting relationships. A colleague worked with a prospect for six years with no results. After year six, he gave them what they needed, and he earned the biggest fee the company ever had.

If you are going to use networking to find mentors, you need to understand a few concepts.

1. You need to understand the dynamics of a mentor – protégé relationship.
2. You have to know what you want to get out of it.
3. You have to understand what makes an appropriate mentor.
4. You need to know how to build relationships.
5. You need to work.

To define a Mentor-Protégé relationship, let's start with what it is not.

- It is not a job hunt. You are not looking for a new boss.
- It is not an opportunity lottery ticket.
- It is not an instant process.

I was thinking about the shortage of Mentor-Protégé relationships, and I labeled it The Undiscovered Relationship. There is a poem by Ella Wheeler Wilcox called The Undiscovered Country. In the poem, she expresses how we explore the world, the external, and ignore our soul, our internal. I find this to be the case with Mentor-Protégé relationships. We take online classes and watch YouTube videos, which are valuable for learning but cannot replace the Mentor-Protégé relationship. Avoiding actions that make you feel vulnerable is supported by pop culture and peer review. Men are supposed to be strong and self-reliant. Women are supposed to be independent. We interpret this pop culture feedback as a call to work alone to be strong and independent.

The Mentor-Protégé relationship is not a dependency nor a tyrant-minion relationship. You should both be strong, self-reliant, and independent. Independent does not mean alone. I have been on teams where the members were strong and independent and others where they were dependent. Each team had people with diverse ideas, a desire to get things done, and were willing to fight for results. The dependent team was continually looking for guidance, presented no new ideas, and had to be pushed to perform. People may picture the Mentor-Protégé relationship as the dependent team, but it only works in an independent team. **Again, independence does not mean alone.**

Life pushes us to believe we can do everything on our own. We have commercials that sell you toothbrushes that work just like the dentist, insinuating we don't need the dentist. We have pills offering an alternative to a healthy diet and exercise. These shortcut products are attractive because we are more "busy" than ever and seek the fast track. The problem is that the fast track doesn't work for everything. A microwaved processed frozen dinner will give you something to eat, but it will not satisfy like a home-cooked meal.

If you are going to achieve big goals, you need homecooked solutions, not frozen TV dinner solutions. The Mentor-Protégé relationship takes work, but it has big payoffs. Since they tend to be hard, many people don't take advantage of these relationships. When I was younger, I had mentors and didn't even know it. They were friends, mostly in volunteer organizations. Some were positive others were destructive. The reason that the relationships were not all good was that I did not have a plan. I did not understand the Mentor-Protégé relationship and followed the loudest rather than the most qualified. The loudest voice can be one of those shiny things we talked about earlier in the book. **Loud does not mean qualified.**

It is easy to get the wrong mentor when you don't have a good idea of your definition of success. If a misguided interpretation of success will skew your goals, it makes sense that it can lead you to the wrong type of mentor.

What further complicates finding a mentor is that successful people are busy and focused, making them difficult to reach and harder to get in front of and build relationships. It would help if you had something to offer. Relationships are two-way streets. You need to be able to offer value to your mentor. Value can be referring business, offering your perspective on topics they are interested in, or performing value adding tasks.

There are many fakers, people who boost themselves as successful with the expensive leased cars, large overleveraged homes, and plenty of time to talk to you. Since you are busy, stressed out, and tired, you see this low-hanging fruit provided by the faker, and you are attracted to that Mentor-Protégé relationship. This relationship has the same effect as the frozen dinner. It fills your belly but does not give you the fulfillment of the home-cooked meal.

An effective Mentor-Protégé relationship takes time and effort to develop. You have to find the mentor, build that relationship and then maintain it.

As I write this book, I want to get even more out of my life. I know where I am now and have set bigger goals, but I am not sure how to achieve them. I have planned my journey through a metaphorical mountain range. I know where I want to go, but I have not personally seen it. I need a guide to help me get there; I need new mentors. I am a senior manager with many established Mentor-Protégé relationships, yet I have trouble finding new mentors. The people I need to talk to are busy, and the onus is on me to find them, as they are not looking for me.

You should approach the mentor search like a job search. Even though you are not looking for a job, use the job search model to show your worthiness. In your job search, you sell yourself to the prospective employer, demonstrating that you have the right attitude and skills for the job and how you would fit into their corporate culture. Apply the same principle when looking for a mentor. If you look for a job through job postings, you are one of the hundreds of applicants. If you know someone at the company, you have a better chance of an interview.

The same is true for mentors. If I were to write a letter to Jack Welch, former chairman of General Electric, asking him to be my mentor, my chance of success would be limited. It would have been a cold call, and he would have no reference to know if I am worth his time. I view this as a lottery ticket chance more than a real opportunity. Instead, I am networking with people I know to gain introductions to the people I want to meet. That connection builds credibility and gives me a better chance of a meeting.

With all of this talk about your worthiness, I want to reiterate that you need to be a worthy protégé, but you need to find a worthy mentor too. Even when you are interviewing for a job, you should be selling yourself, but you should also evaluate the boss and company to make sure they are worthy of you. When seeking a mentor, you should interview them as much as they are interviewing you.

Back to networking! Where do you go to network? It will depend on your interests and your involvement in groups and activities. If you are not involved with any organized groups, you may need to start from scratch, but remember that even your family is a group. To build relationships, you need to join groups, like volunteer organizations, professional organizations, or even religious organizations. Find one that fits your interests. Keep in mind that effective networking requires sincere engagement. If you hate dogs, but the person you want to meet is involved in a dog rescue group, you can't just join the group. The members will see that you are uncomfortable with dogs, and you will not build rapport. Once the dogs come to you and you are reluctant to pet them, they will see you as a faker and an opportunist.

If you work for a sizeable company, they will probably have an association with a major charity organization that could have something that interests you offering an excellent opportunity to get involved and build relationships. Chambers of Commerce are another great resource for networking. There are national volunteer groups like Rotary, Kiwanis; there are skill-building groups like Toastmasters and many other professional organizations you can consider. Never discount religious organizations. If you are religious and active in your religious community, you have the opportunity to network with people who share a common interest. Many people equate golf with networking, but many other sports organizations such as softball or even corn hole (there are some serious corn hole leagues) are places one can network.

The point is to find groups with shared interests. Once you find interest groups, the work begins as you make an effort to build new relationships. Remember, networking is not selling; it is meeting new friends and acquaintances with whom you have something in common. As friends and acquaintances, you are more likely to help each other when asked. It is a process and not a quid pro quo situation. Build relationships, gain associates, and in the future, some of those people will be able to help you, and you will be able to help others. Effective networking goes way beyond business transactions; it is all about relationships.

I am building relationships in my alumni organizations. Typically, alumni organizations help new graduates build relationships with older alumni to get jobs and build mentor relationships. I approached the head of alumni relations to discuss building a program for older alumni, using myself as the prototype.

Recognizing the tremendous need for mentors, I hope the mentoring plan I am working on with the alumni director will show other older alumni that it is not too late to find and use a mentor.

Building the program will add value to the alumni association. The alumni will spread the word about networking and mentoring. I have developed a relationship with the head of alumni relations and have proven that networking will get alumni involved with the university. It helps him as much or more than it helps me.

Once you have proven your worth to your networking partners and they see you as a qualified candidate, it is time to ask for a recommendation.

People fear embarrassment when they recommend someone. They have taken time and effort to build their relationships and don't want to make an introduction that will hurt that relationship. An introduction is an implied recommendation. If you make a networking introduction, you are vouching for that person's character. Let's say that you have an unemployed friend who is a likable person and fun to grab a beer with, but you would never want him to work for you because he is lazy or careless. Would you be willing to recommend him to your boss for a job? You would probably be hesitant. You would be afraid that your friend would embarrass you in front of your boss. Think about how you would feel each time your friend messed something up and your boss looked at you because you recommended him. That is how your network will evaluate you. Will your network be proud to recommend you, or might they be hesitant?

Understanding how people see you will take some self-reflection on how people look at you. Another integral part of the Second Mouse Philosophy is your brand. Your brand is one of the four tools you have right now to help you achieve and is how other people see you. Think about a paper towel commercial. Are you the strong absorbent paper towel, or do you fall apart and push the mess around. How people see you will affect your ability to network effectively and find a qualified mentor.

When you are tired and frustrated, you might want to vent. As you develop mentor relationships, you need to hold off on the negative tirade of all the frustrations you may have; no one wants to listen to a whiner. Most successful people don't want to deal with someone who needs constant guidance. How you present yourself will determine your ability to find the right mentor. Once you build the relationship and have demonstrated that you are a competent protégé, you can be more open with your venting.

You are now cognizant of your personal brand and presenting your best to your network. You are currently involved in groups of people with a common interest and have identified people you want as mentors. You have to ask for introductions at this stage, and it does not need to be specific people. When I talked to the head of alumni relations, I did not have a particular person in mind. He and I had a brainstorming session on what I was looking for and who he knew. After the meeting, we both thought about it and came back with ideas. He had several ideas and made some significant inroads for me. From here, it was up to me to make it work.

You can't expect your network to serve up mentors or other contacts for you; it is your responsibility, and you must take action. You are leveraging their relationships, and you need to build that new relationship. It is time to develop your plan; as you do so, keep these ideas in mind:

- Who – Who do you want to mentor you?
- Why – Why would your prospect want to mentor you?
- What – What do you want them to remember about you when they are making their decision?

When you are looking at developing a mentor relationship, there are three things that I have found that makes a solid mentor-protégé relationship:

1. The mentor is knowledgeable
2. The protégé can build a rapport with the mentor
3. The protégé is open to advice

Finding a knowledgeable mentor can be difficult. Successful people are busy, so you need to put effort into it. You should put together a screening process and look carefully at potential mentors. You are also busy and have no time to waste on a faker. Skipping the screening because you are too busy can lead to more wasted time. If you are going to spend the time to build the relationship, do it with the right person. You don't want the frozen TV dinner version of a mentor when making material changes to your life.

- If the person is too easy to reach or is overly eager to meet, they may have nothing else to do. Fakers will fall all over you and waste your time trying to boost their ego while "mentoring' you. At a conference, I was coaching one of my subordinates on how to network at conferences. He introduced me to a bank vice president who was a nice enough guy, but it was clear he could not help us with our business. I excused myself and signaled my employee that he should end the conversation and move on. He spent another two hours with the guy and missed the opportunity to network with more relevant conference attendees. You don't want to make that mistake when you are trying to get advice on your life.

- Identify the skills and areas on which you need mentoring. You can have a variety of mentors for different parts of your life. For example, I have a career, spiritual, martial arts, and other mentors. Determining your specific needs takes self-reflection and honesty. Where are your weaknesses, and what do you need to improve?
- Networking leads to relationships, so ask people who know the answer. Be choosy on who you ask. I was talking about my need for fitness training, and at that time, I worked with two guys; one was very fit, and the other had a potbelly. The guy with the potbelly was full of fitness advice, with which he was more than willing to regale me. I had to ask the fit person for advice. Which path would you take, the low-hanging fruit of the potbellied person or making an effort to talk to the fit person?
- Get a warm introduction and avoid a cold call. As mentioned earlier, that introduction can give you the credibility needed to open the door. Entering the contact cold means you are a stranger asking for help.
- Set the first meeting. You need to take action, open yourself up, and meet with a stranger to evaluate you as you evaluate them.

When asking for an introduction or giving one, email is the easiest method of communication. The following is an example of what I would send.

Subject: Email Introduction: Joe Mentor – Mike Protégé

Hi Joe,

I met with Mike Protégé the other day. He is someone I think you should meet. He is an up-and-comer who needs some guidance on XYZ. You were the first person that came to mind when we were discussing XYZ.

Mike,

Joe is the person I mentioned when we were discussing XYZ. He has a lot of experience in XYZ, and he is a fascinating person.

I am confident that a meeting will be mutually beneficial. Let me know if you would like me to facilitate a meeting. Otherwise, I will leave it up to you.

Good Luck!

This email gives an introduction, offers help but puts the impetus on the protégé who needs to take some action. You shouldn't spoon-feed people, nor be spoon-fed. Some people will not want to give you this introduction and tell you to "use their name." Contacting someone with the qualifier "Joe Contact recommended I call you." is not as effective as an introduction, but it is better than a cold call.

You will provide many more introductions than you will receive. You need to become a Mentor-Protégé evangelist. Your enthusiasm should be infectious as you start seeing the people around you getting more on board with the concept.

As developed by Napoleon Hill, the Mastermind Group is a group of like-minded people with different skillsets. As you get more people involved in your Mentor-Protégé evangelization, you will build a mastermind group.

This group will magnify your impact on your environment. You will be changing the landscape around you as you sell people on the Mentor-Protégé relationship, expanding your mastermind group. Forming this group benefits all of its members, including you.

The point is that you need to make an effort. No one is going to serve it up for you. You need to want the relationship enough to work for it. You can see that building genuine Mentor-Protégé relationships is not a quick and easy effort. Sometimes qualified mentors will fall into your lap, but that is not the norm.

I attend many classes and seminars. Not only do I learn, but I also observe the teacher, checking if they might be a good mentor. After class, I try to talk to the teacher to at least add them to my network. If they are someone that I would consider for a Mentor-Protégé relationship, I will reach out to meet and discuss the topic they taught. If they are open to the idea, that is the first signal to open to the relationship. Taking the class signaled to them that I am interested in the topic and am willing to spend time increasing my knowledge of it.

I met one of my earliest mentors at a job-hunting seminar hosted by a free job search group. He was a bank president and had some of the skills I needed. After the class, I had the opportunity to chat with him, and I asked if we could continue the conversation. After 25 years, we still keep in touch, and he has insights that still impact my life.

In one memorable session, we were talking about my propensity to work for micro-managers. I was a bit of a pleaser and was sensitive to unreasonable criticism even though I was a high performer. To set the stage, he is small in stature, but he has a strong presence. He is very professional and soft-spoken, so when he said: "Chad, if they don't like you, f*#% them," it shocked me into action. That quick, unexpected comment at that time of my life significantly impacted how I saw the world and set me on a path that led to my future success, including this book.

Make it your mission to seek the people you can work with and give you what you need.

Have you ever had a boss or an extremely competent coworker, but you just couldn't get along with him? How was your relationship? Could you have been more effective if the relationship was better? The same goes for a mentor. It does not matter how qualified someone is; if you don't get along with them, you will have limited success in developing the Mentor-Protégé relationship.

Personality conflicts can be a significant obstacle. If you are competitive and driven, people might see you as a threat or overly aggressive. If you find a person with a noncompatible personality (they are meek/quiet, you are aggressive/strongminded), you will not get the frank feedback you need. Personality differences limit the number of people who can mentor you. Personality conflicts have impacted several areas of my life. I have had bosses who have felt threatened by me, and it has happened in my martial arts training. There have been people I wanted to learn from, but our personalities did not click. I tried to compensate by acting differently, but it came off as fake. These limitations can be discouraging; you can wonder if there is something wrong with you.

Whenever I get discouraged, I reflect on what my bank president mentor told me. "Chad, if they don't like you, f*#% them." Sometimes we need someone else to tell us that it is not us; it is the other person with the problem. The good news is that there are people out there that have the experience you need with whom you can work.

When you build the relationship with your mentor, you develop mutual trust; as you work together, and you will share information in confidence. I have a mentor with whom I used to work. I never reported to him, but we worked on projects together. He has helped me in my career and looks out for me. He has been trying to find the next step in his career, and he gives me updates. I knew about his last two job changes before anyone else. I could have used that information to build political capital with other people in the industry, but I value my relationship more. I kept the information to myself, maintained the trust, and continued building our relationship.

Mentor relationships can last a long time, but it does not mean you have people holding your hand every step of the way. The mentors I have had the longest are ones I don't correspond with often. I talk with them a few times a year, and mostly the contact is social. They still offer feedback, but the relationship has evolved. There comes the point when it is time to let go. In this way, mentoring is similar to parenting. We have an infant that needs a lot of care; a toddler that we need to protect from themselves; children we need to teach; teens we need to guide, and finally, adults we need to let go. This example sounds condescending, but when you put pride away, you see that it fits.

When you have an issue that you can't overcome, you don't know what you don't know. As you interact with the mentor, you gain an understanding of what you need to learn. As you develop the relationship and act on the mentor's feedback, you learn what you need to learn. At that point, the mentor offers guidance as you take what you learn and make it part of your life. As you master the skill, you need less direction and your relationship with the mentor changes.

The interaction between a mentor and a protégé is a relationship, not a transaction. Relationships evolve. Over time trust is built, and the mentor can help you in new and more profound ways. Relationships are two-way streets. You need to show progress and maintain trust. There are times that you will surpass your mentor. Remember the relationship and support them as they supported you. I have had former mentors ask me for advice, and I have given job references to others. If we help each other, we all benefit. Build relationships, and we all benefit.

> **"Sometimes you need to serve in order to lead."**
>
> – ODYSSEUS

You are attracting qualified mentors because you are a qualified protégé. You have skills and the right attitude. You have the potential also to be a great mentor. If you profess the importance of mentorship, what better way can you show your belief than to mentor someone yourself?

If you are a parent, you are a mentor already. You have a protégé in your child. Since the relationship is not by choice, it can be rocky at times, but there may be an opportunity to mentor in your own house.

At work, take a junior person under your wing and help them succeed in their job. Even if you are not a manager, you can help others succeed. By doing so, you are helping the person, helping the company, and in the long run, you are helping yourself.

In martial arts, the final learning step is to teach. Through teaching a skill, you gain a better understanding of the skill yourself. That means when you mentor a person, you will increase your competency in that skill.

I worked with a guy who, at first glance, was someone who I believed could benefit from mentoring. He looked like he was overqualified for his job and just needed a boost to reach his full potential. He worked for a group that did not have effective communication, and his manager gave him unclear objectives. I took him under my wing to see if I could help him get to the next level.

At the outset, I saw some warning signs. First, he was not following through on the tasks we set up. He and I talked, and we set a plan for him to move forward. He had specific tasks that he was to complete but did not put in the work. Second, he would offer to help with menial tasks, which other managers would agree to let him do. He would then complain about being given menial tasks. I talked to him about that, but he did not change his ways.

He was not genuinely interested in improving himself; it seems he was just coming to work to have a job and just wanted to get paid more for the job he was doing. Unfortunately for him, someone who earned half of what he made could do his job. Instead of improving himself to make himself more valuable to the company, he stayed in his comfort zone and put his job at risk by focusing on tasks that less qualified people could complete for a fraction of the salary.

Because he chose this path, he felt constant anxiety. He was fearful of losing his job, and this insecurity pushed him to expound on how (in his mind) the menial work he was doing added value beyond what the company paid him. His complaining and constant overstatement of his importance to the company made it painful to deal with him. Managers and coworkers did not want to deal with him, and as he became more isolated, his anxiety grew. As this happened, he became even more painful.

I gave up on trying to mentor him since he was not open to change. I would listen to him and commiserate to make him feel better, but I spent limited time with him because it was a waste of my time. I was not effective at mentoring him since he was not open to change.

Just like you don't want to waste your time with a mentor who can't teach you, you don't want to spend your time with protégés that can't learn from you. You have limited time; use it as effectively as possible. I felt bad for the guy in the example as he is a good person, and I wanted to help him. If I continued to invest time in him, I would not have had time to coach the woman who wanted to learn and get ahead. She was coachable, so I invested my time in her. She is not perfect, and I get frustrated with her from time to time, but she benefits. I also benefit because I am learning how to be a more empathetic mentor.

The Mentor-Protégé relationship is precious for both parties. If you are not taking advantage of this tool, I recommend you do it. Be vulnerable; open yourself to teach and to learn. You will most certainly have some missteps, but you will find success. In this process, you will learn more than you could on your own, and you will drive success for all the people with whom you are involved.

As you are looking for your mentors, you will find many people who have the experience to offer but just not for you. Keep your eyes open for mentors that could help other people. As I talk to people about mentoring and coaching, I always keep people's needs in mind. I don't have all the answers, and I don't have a strong rapport with everyone I meet. For those I can't mentor, I help find mentors for them.

I know someone who was considering a career in criminal justice. Everything I know about criminal justice is from television and crime novels. I am not a good candidate to mentor this person. I know a few people in the criminal justice field, and I introduced a person who has been a court officer for many years.

It is helping connect people that benefits all parties. Being known as a mentor matchmaker makes you more valuable and will attract people to you. The more you do it; the more likely others are to refer people to you.

I keep talking about helping other people. I am a firm believer in the statement, to lead is to serve. If there is to be a movement or a team, it needs to start with you. The Mentor-Protégé relationship has fallen out of favor, not because it is not practical, but because it gives the appearance of favoritism.

As we overcome the isms in the workplace (racism, sexism, etc.), it is time to bring back the Mentor-Protégé relationship. You may feel like you are on your own as you promote this relationship, and the people around you will continue to follow the inertia of working on their own.

Reflection

Do you want to be effective in networking? How are you going to focus on what they need?

Where will you start networking? What are some other sources for you to network?

What are your goals for networking and for getting a mentor?

Have you ever had people with whom you just couldn't click? How did that affect your ability to work with them?

What are you looking for in a mentor?

What can you do to be a mentorship evangelist?

Takeaways

Have goals, do your homework, and be engaged.

Join an organization because you are interested, and once you are in and involved, you can build relationships. Once you have those relationships in place, you can get introductions.

Everyone needs guidance throughout their life. If you don't need a mentor, you are not growing. Society has an infatuation with role models, putting famous people on pedestals and trying to follow what we believe they stand for, only to be disappointed when they do not meet our expectations. We are surprised and disappointed by role model behavior because we do not know them personally. We project our values to fill in our knowledge gaps and follow a false picture, a person's caricature. Following a role model is an inadequate method of trying to grow. Without a relationship, there is only so much you can do.

When you've found someone, you need to focus on building the relationship. You can't find a prospective mentor and feel you can then unload your whole life on them. If you are in desperate need of advice, consider paying a coach for help. You are paying for their time, so they are expecting you to unload on them. With the mentor, cultivate the relationship and build trust and rapport. If you keep talking about the same thing, you are whining, not getting advice. Also, you need to show results. If you don't act on feedback, the mentor will feel like they are wasting their time.

Results

You are a confident, effective networker. Doing your homework and focusing on the other person attracts more people who want to work with you.

You are growing at a faster rate than you thought possible. Mentors, who guide you, have helped you leapfrog milestones and learn things you could not have achieved alone.

You don't let people hold you back. You accept that some people don't want help and you will not get along with everyone. You remain friendly, but you don't waste your time.

NOTES

NOTES

NOTES

CHAPTER 9
Getting The Most From Your Mentor

In the previous chapter, we discussed how to source, attract and evaluate the mentor. Now what? You have a mentor. What should you do?

You have invested time and energy in sourcing your mentor. Society has indoctrinated us to expect instant results, so you will probably want to see some results, and if you don't get them, you are disappointed. Commercials and access to constant information have reinforced this demand. If results are too slow, there always seems to be a pill, a product, or a process offering quicker results.

You can lose weight faster, you can control your cholesterol, you can bring your product to market, or you can vacuum your home better and faster if you buy their products. A mentor relationship cannot deliver instant results. It is relationship-based, and relationships take time.

If you have children or have been around children, you have probably experienced a seemingly unending series of questions. You feel bombarded and annoyed. The level of tolerance is dependent on your affection for the child; you may be more tolerant with your child than a stranger, but it can drain your patience. You don't want to be that type of annoyance to your mentor. The Mentor-Protégé relationship is not a quick fix. Mentors will guide you but will not provide solutions to your problems. It takes work on your part to make the relationship successful.

Cheese Box

There are two types of growth facilitation, guiding people or providing a solution—coaches and mentors guide, consultants provide solutions. Growth through guidance takes longer but is the more effective route for personal growth.

Guidance – The mentor asks questions and gives suggestions that let the protégé decide on the best course of action. The protégé partners with the mentor, sharing experiences and knowledge which allows the protégé to develop their solution and plan.

Providing Solutions – The consultant develops and provides the solution and plan for the client to follow. It can be harder to take ownership of a plan you have had no involvement in creating for your personal growth.

As with any complicated, long-term project, you should have goals and a plan for your Mentor-Protégé relationship.

- Determine what you want to accomplish.
- What are you expecting from your mentor?
- Does your mentor understand your expectations and willing to accommodate them?

- Do you have an agreed-upon plan with your mentor, including:

  a) Timeline?
  b) Responsibilities?
  c) Actions?

- Do you have a system to measure your success?

It is your life, and the plan is your responsibility; you need to set the tone.

Once you have your goals, document them and share them with your mentor to get feedback. You will get more out of the Mentor-Protégé relationship if the mentor knows what you are trying to accomplish. If your goal is massive, you may not precisely understand what you need to achieve, so your mentor can guide you in finalizing your plan.

Once you have a plan, the essential quality of a promising protégé is a good student. A Zen proverb explains this best.

Once, a long time ago, there was a wise Zen master. People from far and near would seek his counsel and ask for his wisdom. Many would come and ask him to teach them, enlighten them in the way of Zen. He seldom turned any away.

One day an important man, a man used to command and obedience, visited the master. "I have come today to ask you to teach me about Zen. Open my mind to enlightenment." The tone of the important man's voice was one used to getting his way.

The Zen master smiled and said that they should discuss the matter over a cup of tea. When the tea was served, the master poured his visitor a cup. He poured, and he poured, and the tea rose to the rim and began to spill over the table and finally onto the robes of the wealthy man. Finally, the visitor shouted, "Enough. You are spilling the tea. Can't you see the cup is full?"

The master stopped pouring and smiled at his guest. "You are like this teacup, so full that nothing more can be added. Come back to me when the cup is empty. Come back to me with an empty mind."

If you come into a Mentor-Protégé relationship looking for validation of your ideas rather than guidance, you will gain nothing from the relationship, and your mentor will probably get bored with you. The attraction to both parties is that this relationship is a journey where you grow together, sharing personal experiences in an environment of trust. You need to approach it with an empty cup.

Criticism- Friend or Foe? As with many other things, your biggest obstacle is generally in your head. We all want criticism when we ask for it; we are less receptive when we actually receive it. When I was editing my first book, I asked five successful business people to read the manuscript and give feedback. I wanted it; I needed it, but when I got it, I was shocked. The manuscript I had put almost a year of effort into was not as perfect as I thought. I received criticism that I asked for, it was constructive and accurate, but it felt unfair. After all of this work, how could it not be complete? How could it still have flaws?

I had to remind myself that I asked them for feedback.

- I wanted negative feedback so I could make the book better.
- I had to fight every instinct to be defensive.
- I had to fight to open myself up.
- I had to admit to myself and others that it needed improvement.

We all have this struggle in one form or another. We want to be self-sufficient. We want the respect of others, and we want to be right. When we open ourselves up for evaluation and feedback, we strip away those feelings, and it can make us feel defensive.

Feeling dependent on other people can make you anxious and out of control. Like most people, I like being in control. For example, I hate being late and being at the mercy of someone else driving makes me a little anxious. I was traveling with one of the firm's partners, and he wanted us to drive together to the airport. We do not have the same sense of time. I like to get to the airport early, settle in, and work while waiting to board. He prefers to work in the office and doesn't think a time buffer is necessary. We left for the airport about an hour later than I would have left. We hit traffic, and we got to the airport while they were boarding our flight. I was anxious; he was fine.

You may feel uncomfortable, even anxious, when you hear advice from your mentors, but getting others to help you improve is not adding a dependency. You are not losing control by working with someone who is giving you feedback. That is not to say there aren't people who will try to control you. That is why I emphasize the need to evaluate your mentor before building the relationship. This relationship is yours to develop.

- You need to have a guide, not a tyrant.
- You are looking to improve.
- You have control.
- You get to choose to whom you listen.

When you show your flaws, you feel that other people will not respect you. Respect can feel like a competition. A common belief is that you earn respect and can lose people's respect with one misstep. To be vulnerable and to open yourself to criticism is not a respect-diminishing act and wanting to improve is not a weakness. Receiving constructive criticism is not a form of disrespect. It can feel that way, especially if the person is not skilled at delivering criticism. The one caveat is that you don't want to open yourself up to just anybody, like airing your dirty laundry on Facebook. In this relationship, you are working with people you trust and want you to succeed. They are not disrespecting you by giving you negative feedback.

We have an innate need to be right, and insecurity and a need to maintain a positive sense of self can lead to feelings of disrespect. Our egos don't want to hear that we need improvement, and this resistance to feedback is extreme when we have a lot of experience. I am currently struggling with feedback on my career direction. Several mentors tell me that I should make some material changes, but their guidance makes me feel like I am giving up 25 years of experience to do something else. In reality, I am not giving up a lifetime of experience; I will use the skills I have built over the years, just in a different way.

There will be a conflict between you relying on your experience and your desire for growth. Your experience, although valuable, causes inertia that keeps you moving down a path. A desire for growth wants you to move to a different path. This conflict can stall you like a tug of war in a stalemate.

Experience is like an outdoor hot tub in a snow storm. You run through the cold and get into the hot tub. The tub feels uncomfortably hot, but you get used to it. Once you are used to it, the air feels cuttingly cold, and you submerge your body with just your head sticking out. When you want to do something else, you start to get out, the cold cuts through you, and you get back in. It can be challenging to get out without a strong reason. That is why many people don't career plan until they lose their jobs.

We spend time looking for a mentor; we carefully evaluate to ensure we get along, we build the relationship, and then the mentor gives you negative feedback. What a rip-off! They are not basking in our greatness. Can't they see our experience? It takes effort to get out of the hot tub (comfort zone), brave the cold air (uncomfortable feedback), and benefit from mentoring. When you accept that you want and need to grow, you will have to open yourself up to uncomfortable conversations and accept the feedback that will lead to growth.

You can compare self-improvement to forging metal. I once took a blacksmithing class, and I found it enlightening. You start with a plain bar of metal. You heat the metal until its structure changes, so it is malleable. You can't get it too hot, or you will burn the metal. (I didn't realize that could happen to steel). You then hammer the steel on an anvil and change its shape. To transform the steel bar into a tool puts the steel through tremendous stress, and you need to take the stress out of the steel to make it useful.

You put yourself in the metaphorical forge when you enter a Mentor-Protégé relationship. Instead of heat, you use vulnerability to make yourself malleable. The mentor is the hammer that impacts you to change. Think of the expression we all use, "that person had a huge impact on me" As you are changing, you go through stress. To continue the analogy; if you have too much heat (go too fast or have a solution without ownership), you burn the steel; you burn yourself out. If you build up too much stress, like the steel gets brittle, you feel pent-up anxiety. I have experienced this. It is a good sign when you don't believe in the solution yet but move forward anyway. The hard part is determining if you have the wrong solution or if you are too rigid.

I have studied both traditional and non-traditional styles of martial arts for many years. I am currently studying a traditional Okinawan style. When I started, like the visitor to the Zen master, I had a full cup. I already had two other black belts, and I began this new style as a white belt with a black belt attitude. I came to class carrying a mantle of experience rather than seeking personal growth.

My martial arts experience was different in some fundamental ways from what I was learning now, and the teacher was constantly correcting me, which hurt my ego. I saw the value of learning this new style, and I wanted to learn it, but my cup was full. My mind told me, "you have two black belts; why do you need to learn more. Just keep on doing it the old way." For months, I had negative self-talk, "You don't need to learn new things." It was difficult for me. It wasn't until I had some breakthroughs that I emptied my cup, opened myself up to criticism, and made myself vulnerable. It was that vulnerability that allowed me to grow. Martial Arts teaches humility, but that is one of the more challenging lessons.

Another black belt in my school took it upon himself to help me out. He had a similar martial arts background and had experienced some of the same difficulties with this style. Understanding the challenges, having experienced them himself, he saw that I was a serious student, so he invested his time in helping me. He became a mentor. He had a skill I need, we had a rapport, and he wanted me to grow.

We all want to make people we care about feel better and don't like to point out flaws. Your mentor is no different, so you may need to encourage criticism. As I mentioned before, I needed help editing my first book and had to be open to criticism. To accomplish this, I needed to make people feel good about criticizing me as they were helping me improve my work. It still felt like a direct criticism of me. You may need to mentor the mentor on how they can provide criticism effectively, thus coaching them on their feedback skills.

Remember, you asked your mentor for help. They may not have the best bedside manner, and you need to give them feedback on how you are responding to their feedback. If you did your vetting well and know the person has your best interests in mind, don't end the relationship because they hurt your feelings. Let them know how you feel. You can't maximize the relationship if you are not open with each other. Honesty will improve your experience.

Your mentor is not a service provider; they are helping you without compensation, and you should show your appreciation. You can do this by sharing your expertise in other areas, helping them become better mentors, and helping them with their business.

I always make a point to reciprocate and share my knowledge with my mentors and coaches. A great example is my personal trainer. I was never a sports person, so I never had fitness training other than a gym class. She helps me with my fitness, teaches me the proper technique, and pushes me when my brain gives up before my body is ready to stop. She has specific expertise that I don't have but desperately need. She was considering the next step in her career, and I shared my experience and offered guidance.

You can also add value to someone who has more experience than you. I have several business mentors who help me with career advice and advice on specific projects. You may be wondering how I could help someone who has more experience than me in my profession. In this case, I helped one of my mentors with social media. He knew he should be more active on LinkedIn but did not know the in's and out's. I took him on a tour of my LinkedIn page and discussed how to share content and improve his online presence.

Suppose you have valuable experience and the opportunity to help your mentor. Don't push your expertise on your mentor; make sure only to provide advice that is welcome. You want to add value, and not everyone is open to learning from a protégé. If you get the sense that your mentor may get annoyed, don't push. You need to build the relationship, and your mentor needs to know you and understand your talents before you will have the credibility required to offer advice.

Just as you need to determine with whom you share your goals, you need to be selective when sharing your expertise. As a black belt in other styles, I am a bit of a "teacher" in my presentation. I need to hold that back because I am not an expert in this style. When I show the higher belts my new info, I do it more to learn more, not to teach them something. An example is a block that I learned in a seminar. It took so little energy that it felt fake and did not seem possible to work. As I shared this with the higher belt, he opened up and showed me more to perform the move even better.

As discussed in the last chapter, one of the easiest ways to help your mentor is through introductions. In your search for a mentor, you have been networking. You have met many people and understand a bit about who they are and what they need. You can be a matchmaker. Suppose your mentor needs or sells a service; you may know people who can be a match. One of my coaches teaches business-related classes and is always looking for leads. I initiated introductions to businesses that could benefit from his classes. After the introduction, he would take it from there. I have also been able to arrange speaking engagements for other mentors.

I have also been the recipient of this kind of reciprocity. I am coaching a woman on how to work in an office environment. Her previous work was outside the office environment, working with vendors. She needed help assimilating into her new environment. She reciprocated by introducing someone who could advise me on marketing my books and facilitating a big presentation.

To build a solid relationship, you need to know each other's needs and support each other appropriately. When you are sharing information with your mentor, determine why you are doing it. Are you sharing because the information is valid and welcomed, or are you sharing it to put your knowledge on display? The latter highlights your insecurity and does not help your mentor.

You don't need to prove your worth constantly. Showing how smart you are is a defense mechanism to hide insecurity. Be vulnerable and open yourself up to get the most out of your Mentor-Protégé relationship. Don't hide behind the know-it-all wall. It is okay if you can't teach your mentor anything, as it is not a prerequisite to the Mentor-Protégé relationship, just a potential value add. You can add value in other ways.

A reminder that you pay coaches, not mentors. Mentor relationships take time to develop. Coaches are almost instant. If you need help right now, a coach can give you specialized help while building and growing your mentor relationships.

Just as you would with a mentor, you need to vet potential coaches. Unless you are joining the circus, you don't want a clown as a coach. You want a qualified person with whom you have a rapport. The shortcut comes in that you can unload on the coach immediately because you are paying them to listen. Examples of coaches are personal trainers, career and executive coaches, writing coaches, spiritual directors, marriage and family counselors, financial advisors (Ramsey, etc.), psychologists and psychiatrists, nutritionists, and teachers.

Be a good student, be open to learning, and add value to your mentor or coach when you can.

Once you have built some experience, you can then start mentoring in your target area. To be an effective mentor, you need to be confident; if you doubt your skills and don't believe your message is valuable, you will not be an effective mentor. Think about a time when you were listening to a presentation. If the person did not speak with confidence, did you pay much attention? If the person did not seem to believe their message, what did you believe?

I have had the opportunity to interact with many people in different situations. People who can speak with confidence always have an easier time spreading their message. If you are going to be a mentor, you need to be confident in delivering your message.

One of my most memorable mentors is a retired bank president I have known for 25 years. He projects confidence. When I say that, you may think it means he is pushy and loud, but it is precisely the opposite. He is calm, quiet, and professional, but the way he presents himself personifies confidence. His confidence is one of the reasons he is such a good mentor. When he speaks, people listen.

Confidence also brings knowing when not to mentor. People must want to improve for there to be value-added; a mentor shouldn't chase people around. As you grow, you will encounter people with great potential; you will want them to succeed, but you will just waste your time trying to help them if they do not want to help themselves.

I have experienced this more times than I have built Mentor-Protégé relationships. There is so much potential, but people don't want to take advantage of it. You cannot force them to grow, even though you see what they could achieve if they tried.

It is easy to get caught up trying to get people to listen to you. The people around you may not see you as a mentor. If you have grown, they may still see you as the person you were; they may be comfortable with where they are and may have different objectives.

As a mentor, your job is to help people achieve their dreams and goals. You do not want to become an influencer projecting your goals onto them. When I was younger, I went to a barber who cut hair that matched his. I would ask for a style, and I would always leave looking not quite right. After looking at people leaving the barber, I noticed that the barber's style bled through to all his customers. I changed barbers.

There will always be some bleed-over of style and goals, which is why it is essential to have a rapport with your protégé. You need to share some values to be successful. Think about politicians in a Mentor-Protégé relationship. Could a staunch conservative mentor a progressive liberal in how to win a political election? Let's say that the extreme conservative is the best at winning elections, and the radical liberal is a good student. Would this be a productive Mentor-Protégé relationship? Probably not. There is a chance that it would work if both participants are very open to other views. Still, if they are genuinely radicals, philosophical differences would probably create a wall between them that would be insurmountable. There will be people with great potential who may be excellent students, but if your values are polar opposite, it would not be an effective Mentor-Protégé relationship.

When mentoring, do not lose sight that your time is valuable; you have your goals to accomplish and things you need to learn. You do not have time to waste on people who do not want to grow. You may feel lousy cutting out your unproductive proteges, but if you spend your time with someone who does not want to grow, you miss the opportunity to mentor someone who does want to grow. Leaving the unproductive protégé behind doesn't leave them worse off because they don't want to grow anyway. There remains the chance that your decision wakes them up and pushes them to start growing.

As we get older, many feel that we outgrow the mentor protégé relationship and believe that it should be between an older and a younger person. The person just graduating from college or is new to the workforce. We see mentor programs for disadvantaged youth. For a more senior person, the Mentor-Protégé relationship can feel like you are sitting in the little chair looking up at the teacher, like in grammar school. That is pride speaking; your ego saying you are strong and independent and can succeed on your own. If you open yourself up and allow yourself to be vulnerable, you will find yourself able to ask for guidance and to grow more than you ever could on your own.

Reflection

What are you willing to do to invest time and effort into your Mentor-Protégé relationships?

What are your goals for each of your Mentor-Protégé relationships?

What obstacles to learning do you have? What can you do to be more open to criticism?

How can you gain the confidence you need to mentor others?

Takeaways

The Mentor-Protégé relationship does not offer instant results.

Change is never an easy task. You can experience tremendous growth with a productive Mentor-Protégé relationship.

- Find a trustworthy, qualified mentor.
- Build a mutually beneficial relationship.
- Be open to change.
- Always remember that you are in control.

Having the right mentor will open your eyes to possibilities you did not know existed.

When you are mentoring others, you need to be confident in your topic.

Your time is valuable. Get the most out of your relationships.

Results

You have leapfrogged your previous accomplishments, and you have helped others leapfrog theirs.

You have utilized your mentors by setting goals, setting expectations, having a plan, and being patient.

You can accept and utilize criticism. By accepting your vulnerability, you have mitigated your anxiety.

You have reached a higher level because you have started mentoring others. Fully understanding the role of a mentor allows you to work with your mentors even more effectively.

You have also retained your humility. You only mentor on subjects for which you have expertise.

NOTES

NOTES

NOTES

CHAPTER 10
Build Your Mentor Team

Another major tenant of the Second Mouse Philosophy is the importance of your team. Your team includes people all around you, family, friends, coworkers and service providers. We recategorize them to build your mentor team.

- Your Sponsors – the people who offer you opportunities.
- Your Mentors/Coaches – The people who advise you.
- Your Peers – The people at your level.
- Your Subordinates – The people whom you sponsor or mentor.

From this group, you can build your Mentor Team with your mentors and protégés. Your team can be broad and will add value and satisfaction to your life.

I have a pretty big mentor team. I have a career/life coach, several career mentors, a fitness trainer, and several martial arts mentors. I recently added a speaking coach and am looking to add a spiritual director to the mix. As a mentor, I currently have two writing protégés, a career protégé, and a speaking protégé who provide me with as much value as I offer them. Along with gaining the help I need to succeed, I have built friendships and grown as a person.

It is vital to lead by example. You can demonstrate the value of mentorship by being a mentor. If you feel insecure with your ability to mentor, mentor in a place where you feel most comfortable. No matter what you do, you will find mentor opportunities to mentor someone who wants to learn and grow.

What makes you a good mentor? Think about what you were looking for in your mentors; qualified people with whom you could build a rapport. To be qualified means you need to have experience in your field of expertise, and you need to be approachable.

Don't stretch yourself outside of your area of expertise; we are all experts in something. You can get excited about helping someone who needs guidance and is open to learning, and you want to fill the role of mentor. If you are not an expert, they will pick it up, and the longer it takes, the deeper the hard feelings will be. Don't negative self-talk yourself out of mentoring; use my example. I have had to work with IT departments to develop software and know some things about software development. But because I do not know the specifics, I would be doing my protégé a disservice. In this case, I would refer the prospective protégé to an expert in software development rather than attempting to do this myself.

Does that mean I have nothing to offer in that arena? No. I have experience in a segment of software development. I can mentor the business sponsor on interacting with IT personnel and teaching strategies to keep projects on track. That is where my expertise lies. I am not a software expert, but I do have project management experience within the field.

You need to look at your experience the same way. Where does your expertise lie? You have it. You have lived a life that has taught you lessons. Even if you had a disadvantaged upbringing and are just starting in your career, you have experience. You can mentor kids who are experiencing an underprivileged childhood. You can show them that they can be successful.

You also need to be approachable; I have trouble in this area. I can be very intense; I am on the large side and a direct communicator. I had a habit of shunning vulnerability, withholding my feelings and a culturally driven idea of strength. These characteristics have made it hard for others to communicate with me.

I have focussed on having more empathy. Having empathy does not mean that I feel bad for people. (that is sympathy) I am focusing on seeing the world from the perspective of others. My empathy has helped me open up and become more comfortable with being vulnerable in a mentor/coaching relationship.

As I opened up and showed vulnerability, I became more approachable. It goes back to the personal brand. I hired a resume coach who did not just rearrange my experience on a piece of paper. He had me poll my bosses, my peers, and my subordinates on their views on me. He believed that others could better describe me, and I found this to be true. It gave me a strong understanding of my professional brand. Below is the result of his poll.

Confident, technically-oriented and resourceful STRATEGIC INITIATIVES EXECUTIVE with a proven track record of success. Creative problem solver, who thrives on challenges, is cool under pressure and gets the job done. Bright, analytical and competitive team player who possesses outstanding interpersonal and communication skills. Strong participatory leader and coach, organized and thorough planner, and win/win negotiator dealing effectively across all levels of the organization. Accustomed to a fast pace and multiple projects, fulfills priorities and understands competing agendas while consistently achieving customer and project objectives.

That is resume speak, but it gives you an idea of who I am from others' perspectives. It is my professional personal brand. If you read into it, you'll see primary is problem-solving and getting results, and secondary is coaching. It shows that I can have an intensity that might intimidate newer employees or insecure people, meaning that I might not be the best person to coach a brand new person in the workforce. I will benefit people who have more experience and want a steady hand to help them move forward.

Look at your personal brand. If you can, take one of those professional personality tests to get an understanding of your brand. If you can survey how people see you, that would be even better. Once you understand how approachable you are, you can adjust your approachability or limit your protégé pool to people you currently have a rapport with.

Beyond experience, you need some skills to be an effective mentor. Those skills include:

1. **You need to be a good listener.** It means active listening. You need to ask questions to get people to tell you the real story.
2. **Be a guide.** Help your protégé come up with the answers themselves. You offer guidance, and they find their path.
3. **Don't be an influencer.** Avoid projecting your goals and dreams on your protégé. Guide, don't push. Your protégé is not a junior version of you.

You can see this in action when you watch children's sports. We have parents who support their kids, allow them to have fun, and guide them to high performance. On the other side, we have parents living vicariously through their kids. These parents push the kids to do things that they can't or won't do themselves. As a mentor, you will benefit your protégé if you emulate the first set of parents.

In the age of craftsmen, there was the position of the apprentice. The expert would take on an apprentice to learn side by side. They would do the menial work so the craftsman could work to his highest and best potential while teaching the apprentice his craft. The world seems to have moved away from this, and if a company has succession planning, it is generally quite sterile.

The pendulum swung away from mentorship because it can give the impression of favoritism as the mentor puts their energy into a protégé at others' expense. You have to weigh up between what is better for the company and the appearance of fairness. When considering protégés, you need to be inclusive and make sure that you don't end up with a primarily male protégé network if you have a predominately male leadership team.

A sterile succession plan causes a loss of experience and information. The sterile plan puts employees into groups of individuals who are generally working in the same direction but are not coordinated or guided toward their goals. There is only so much you can learn without guidance, and you can not be a real team without opening up to one another.

A leader or someone that appears to be a leader sticks out like a beacon in the darkness, constantly attracting people. There is a hunger for leadership and teams, but the sterile plan pushes everyone apart, offering a mere illusion of fairness. It provides no support or opportunities for people as they grow. You can see the dissatisfaction of supportive workplaces on social media.

I coach men and women. Mentor relationships between a variety of people from different backgrounds can be very effective.

Now is an excellent time to catalog your accomplishments and experiences. If you are like me, you achieve things, celebrate them, and move along. You are onto the next thing, leaving your accomplishment in the dust.

It is good to be forward-focused and not rest on past achievements, but it is vital to remember and document those accomplishments. We usually struggle to update our resumes. If you have been with the same company for five to ten or more years, you can struggle to try to think back to remember what you've achieved.

Reviewing your accomplishments a few times a year is a good confidence booster and keeps your resume nimble if something catastrophic happens at your company. Looking at and cataloging your achievements and experiences reminds you that you can accomplish goals. We all have times of feeling insecure. Looking back at your accomplishments is the best medicine; it is energizing to remember what you can achieve.

Another benefit of cataloging your accomplishments is to recognize the areas where you can help others. Consider all aspects of your life, not just your work-life. You can mentor people on how to get fit after having a heart attack or bouncing back from a bad relationship. It can be work-related in helping others with how to become the top salesperson or succeed in turnaround management. As you mentor people, you might find that you can charge for your services and coach instead. If you have a skill in demand, you can coach others as a side gig.

Rapport is vital as you need to communicate with other people. If you can't convey your message, it does not matter how compelling your message is. People need to understand your message for it to be beneficial to them.

Communication is like any other skill that needs practice, and mentoring people you know well is a good start. You can consider communication classes, and there are numerous books on how to hone your message. As I've mentioned a few times before, Toastmasters is a great place to help develop your public speaking skills. As you focus on public speaking and leadership and improve, you will find that you improve in your other areas of communication simultaneously.

How do you attract potential protégés or clients if you are looking to get paid? Offering presentations on your topic is your best bet. If you can talk to organizations that focus on your skill, you will reach your target audience.

You want to get your name into the market. Start networking in different circles and get active on social media. As I promoted my book and held speaking engagements, I would post content on social media. This promotion increased my network size, which helped sell my book and bring more attention to me and my activities. People started approaching me to ask for mentoring or coaching.

Many of these meetings turned out to be question sessions or a couple of meetings that petered out. That is okay. Not everyone is ready to be mentored, even if they think they are. I keep in touch to see how they are doing, and they have become great networking partners. It remains a win-win relationship.

You have your expertise, and now you are spreading the word and sharing your knowledge. It will help you not only in your quest to be a mentor but also in your job, networking, getting new jobs, and getting side gigs. Even if your mentoring skill has nothing to do with your job, you become a better communicator; you show you are a complete person and not an automaton that does their job and goes home. Being a mentor gives you as much, if not more than it provides your proteges.

Since the mentor's value is not understood and even shunned by some that would call it favoritism or an old boys type network, you need to show the value. By being a mentor to others, you can demonstrate the value of the mentor relationship.

It demonstrates that the mentor grows through the Mentor-Protégé relationship. You just have to get the message out.

Talking about the benefits of the Mentor-Protégé relationship is essential, as, in many instances, you will be starting from scratch. With fewer gatekeepers (administrative staff), the wall you have to climb is now even higher. Before, you could build relationships with assistants and secretaries, and they would become the bridge to the person you are targeting.

With the gatekeeper's elimination because of budget cuts, one would think it is easier to get in touch with people. Sadly, it is just the opposite. People just don't return calls or reply to emails. Communication seems to vanish into a black hole. If you are going to get what you need, you need to shine.

As a successful mentor, you can be a beacon and shine in the eyes of those who want to grow and want to help others grow.

A mentor team is a group of individuals with one connection point, unlike a traditional team with everyone in their place working toward a team goal. It is a group of individuals, directly and indirectly, striving for an individual's success.

The key to the mentor team's success is each individual's success, which is a little counter-intuitive. Most teams have a collective goal for which all the team members strive as a unit. The mentor team's purpose is to support each member in the achievement of their individual goal.

The mentor team members do not work together, and the group is held together by you. These people may never interact, but I tend to introduce my team members to each other, but you don't have to.

The mentor team seems to break the stereotype of what a team should be. Is it really a team at all? This team is the only one in which "I" has a place. We are looking for individual advancements while supporting each other in this endeavor.

When building your team, you need to avoid the psychological phenomenon called groupthink. Your team should not comprise people precisely like you. If your team is not diverse, you are limiting yourself. It is easier to deal with people just like you, but you miss out on different perspectives.

You need to build a good rapport within the team. While you can't have anyone belligerently against you, civil discourse on topics is vital for personal growth.

Cheese Box

Diversity

Having a diverse team will give you more opportunities for success.

We are used to global influence moving from west to east and from north to south. That is changing, and we see influence flow in the opposite direction. Having a diverse team will give you access to different perspectives and ideas. Having access to those perspectives and ideas give you a leg up on your peers in identifying opportunities. Besides opportunities, you can gain more empathy and understanding for others. Embracing diversity will not only open you up for growth but open you up to helping others grow.

I mentioned it before, and I will repeat it because it is crucial. You take on the characteristics of those around you. You cannot choose your family, and you don't always choose who you work with or for; for your team, you need to intentionally build a group that positively influences you and help you get ahead while assisting them.

This idea is not new. As discussed earlier, Napoleon Hill, in his top-rated book, "Think and Grow Rich," talks about forming a mastermind group. "Think and Grow Rich" was written in 1937, so this concept has been around for a long time. Building the mastermind group takes a lot of work, so most people don't bother even starting, causing us to get caught in the inertia of sticking with the people around us.

Suppose you follow the path of least resistance; yes, you get farther faster because there is no resistance. But what if you are on the wrong path? If you are leading people to a new process, you can't succeed following the path of least resistance; you must make changes. A great start to that change is building your support group. A mentor team is a support group on steroids. You are not just getting help; you are building a success engine.

The people you mentor are just as important as the people who mentor you. Many of these people will become your peers. I once thought I was just helping someone and did not recognize that it was a mentor-protégé relationship. It was someone who worked for me, and I was giving guidance. Looking back on it now, I was a mentor, and he was a protégé.

I strive for my work team members to grow and become my peers. If people see my team as the path to growth and success, I will attract the best of the best to my team. I was once mentoring a strong member of my team. He listened and did well. I hit a major career setback, and he and I became peers sooner than expected, causing us to become rivals more than allies for a while. We lost touch when I moved on. Years later, he reached out to me, and we had a great conversation. Our relationship evolved into peers who now wanted to help each other succeed. This story's point is that the team's path can be winding and will separate but may end up helping you years later.

Your protégé will not be a subordinate forever; the objective is for them to grow. As they move on, they may become your peers or even sponsors in the future.

I started at a company and was reporting to a lady who was new to leadership. She was competent, and we got along well. As the company grew, I was offered an opportunity in another area, and we became peers. After some changes and another growth opportunity for me, she became my subordinate. The company offered me a transfer, she took my job, and we were peers again.

You don't know how your team will be structured in the future; be conscious of your interaction with all levels. You need to build a strong and flexible team.

Success is never a straight line to the top. As your life cycles through times of greater and lesser success with many ups and downs, you need to continue growing and adding to your network. Think of your success as a mountain road. It meanders back and forth until you reach the peak.

As you travel this road, you need to go to new areas on your map. Each area of the map is fresh, and you may need guidance as you change. The higher you go up the mountain, the harder it becomes to change.

When you are struggling and need help, a trusted advisor who can act as a sounding board can help you through the tough times. Having that independent opinion is more powerful than having a friend or loved one guide you. Your loved ones may just try to make you feel better.

You should also serve as an independent advisor to others. As your protégés or mentors experience challenges, you need to be there for them. As a mentor team, we help each other.

It is vital to maintain a fresh and valuable team. You may have a team member who gives nothing and is a taker; you might have someone who turns out to be negative or someone who misrepresented themselves. You want a strong team, so it is essential to cull these people. You do not have the time or energy to deal with anyone who will suck the life from you.

Just as you should do regular self-assessments, you should have regular assessments of your team. Is your team producing for you? If not, you need to determine why. Is it because you are not feeding your team? If you do not give your team a reason to help you, you can't expect their help.

I cut an author from my team. We wrote our books around the same time. We had a discussion and agreed to give each other leads to market our books. As we had agreed, I read and reviewed his book online. I am a fast reader, so I was not concerned when I did not see his review. I referred several people to his business, one of whom became a customer. I referred him to a national podcaster specializing in his topic, and he got a spot on the podcast. Eight months later, no review on my book and not one lead despite posting activities that apply to my book and could have benefit me. Our books do not compete; they complement each other. He has proven himself to be a taker, so he is cut.

Another company executive tries to help but does not have the pull he thinks he does and contributes to a point. He has helped me in the past but not enough to justify my effort to maintain the relationship. I still keep in touch with him, but I put him on the B team. I socialize and give him leads but never expect much in return.

There are some team members you just need to accept for who they are. One, in particular, has helped me get jobs and given me good advice. He tends to go ghost on me regularly. I drop him notes every once in a while and have learned not to be upset when he doesn't respond.

Build and maintain your team. Make sure your team is productive. You only have so much time and energy. Maximize your efforts.

Reflection

Who is on your mentor team right now? They don't need to be formal relationships.

In what areas do you need guidance?

In what areas can you share your experience?

Are you ready to lead by example, mentor others, and seek out mentors for yourself?

Do you have empathy? What can you do to gain more empathy?

Do you project an image that attracts potential mentors and protégés?

How can you return the favor to your mentors?

Takeaways

Your mentor team is a crucial part of your team.

You will need to be a champion for the Mentor-Protégé relationship.

You need to be aware of your personal brand. You have a lot to offer prospective protégés.

When you are mentoring, be a guide, not an influencer.

Don't be afraid to cut unproductive or destructive people from your team.

Results

You empower yourself while empowering others. You are learning and growing at an unprecedented rate, reaping the fruits of your labor.

People see you as someone they want to work with, a beacon for mentorship, and they look to you for guidance and positive thoughts.

You have developed an environment of constant growth, and people are attracted to you.

NOTES

NOTES

NOTES

Executing The Plan – Avoid The Trap And Get The Cheese

Here we are at the end of the book. What's next? Action is essential. Your success will not start with sitting on the couch, watching reruns. You need to execute your plan.

What have you done so far?

1. You have identified your definition of success.
2. You have set goals based on that definition.
3. You have identified the skills, information and experience you need to achieve your goals.
4. You are getting the information you need to succeed.
5. You are networking (talking to people) to identify people who have the skills you need.
6. You are building your teams.
7. You are building relationships with the people in your teams (mentors and coaches).

You can take action now, even if you haven't completed all of the steps. There are plenty of things you can do to start reaching your goals. You can pursue the above steps parallel to maintaining your regular duties. Remember, you don't need to hold off your plans until you get mentors or coaches.

A good example is my writing. I write outside of my typical workday. For my first book, I acted without following all of the steps above. Writing a book is only the beginning of the work when your goal is actually to publish a book. There is so much more that goes into the book after you write it.

As I was writing, I networked to find the experts and reached out to get introductions to people to gain some much-needed information. With that information, I changed how I used the book. Instead of the book being the product, I used it to increase my personal brand.

When you start writing, you have dreams of best sellers and people seeking you out. That is not the reality; unless you are a celebrity. You need to do most of the legwork to promote your book. I had to make a decision. Do I want to market the book, or do I want to market my personal brand?

I chose to market my personal brand, moving my book from a product to a tool. I still sell the book as it is a product, but it is also a tool and is part of the Chad Betz product line. That product line includes my day job, the book, and any coaching or consulting I do on the side.

I learned as I was taking action. I spoke to a best-selling author on how I should market the book, an author who uses the book as a tool for his business, the owner of one of the top independent bookstores in America and many people who self-published. They all contributed to my plan by adding their experience, which enhanced my own and helped me succeed. I made many mistakes, but I learned, and I made progress.

The process is never perfect; you will miss some steps, but you will learn and compensate. To continue the example of my first book, I learned that an author should start publicizing their book for around six months before publishing. The problem was, I learned this a month after I published my book.

Learning something this important after you have committed can be a point of distress. You may think you have had a catastrophic screw-up, and you might consider stopping. When I learned about pre-marketing a book, I felt that pressure. I felt insecure and questioned my trying to publish on my own. How could I have missed this?

I reflected on it myself and talked to my coach. I had to step back and think about the real impact. I intended to use my book to improve my personal brand. How was that going?

1. People were buying my book. That is a positive.
2. People were coming to my presentations. That is a positive.
3. I learned that next time I could get even more publicity if I start publicizing before I publish. That is a positive.

Could I have had more success if I started publicizing before I published? Maybe. I worked in parallel, and I published a book. I used what I learned and followed a better process to publish this book.

I used mentors and coaches to push me forward. They are accountability partners to avoid holding off on execution. There are traps throughout the process. As you learn and discover there is more to learn, you have the feeling that you need to stop and not move forward. You need to have the faith to believe in yourself and your goals.

You will never have all the information you need when making a decision; make some assumptions when you start and trust that you will find answers along the way.

It is easy to get crippled by a lack of information. A lack of information can cause anxiety. You can address that anxiety through thoughtful planning and action.

> *"You often feel tired, not because you've done too much, but because you've done too little of what sparks a light in you."*
> — ALEXANDER DEN HEIJER.

A good example is a toxic work environment. I worked for a company that had a strange mix of micromanagement, indecision, and inaccessibility. Employees were required to get approval for even the most minor decisions. Management was slow in their decision-making and would reject plans and continually ask for more information. They tended to sequester themselves in conference rooms, causing backlogs in the approval process, exacerbating the problem.

People were striving to get recognition, to earn the trust that would never come, as the culture developed in which people felt it was their fault that plans weren't getting done. They questioned themselves, their ability to gain the right information and correct answers - leaving everyone drained and tired.

The company set unachievable targets, making the employees feel like they were failing. The managers were generally nice and likable people who earned people's loyalty. I felt bad for them. Those managers have such an extreme fear of missing out that they spend 12 to 14 hours a day trying to approve every decision, no matter how small. They discussed pushing the decision power down the chain to scale but always panicked and pulled decision-making back to within their control. Being overly focused on these approvals, they missed the opportunity to drive the company and scale the operations strategically.

This story shows two forms of inaction: the employees and the managers.

The employees are stuck in the hamster wheel. They keep running without getting anywhere and not understanding why. They blame themselves and feel stressed out and tired. They feel like they are taking action because they are working, but they do not take action for their goals. Work that does not help you achieve your goal is inaction. And it is destructive inaction because it leaves you feeling discouraged and makes it harder to achieve your goals.

Management's fear of missing out causes their inaction. Worrying that someone will miss something, they are willing to let time-sensitive plans sit until they feel they have all of the information. Because we seldom have all of the information, they finally panic and make poorly thought-out last-minute decisions.

I work just as hard as they do. I typically start my day around 5:00 AM and keep going to 9:00 PM. The difference is that I add in my goals.

5:00 AM – working out.

6:00 AM - writing

8:00 AM to 6:00 PM – day Job.

7:30 PM – Martial Arts class, presentation for my book or other classes.

In other words, I focus on my goals just as much as I focus on my day job.

Have you felt that you just don't want to go to workout, but you did and felt so good afterward? Working on your goals gives you the same energized feeling. I like to write in the morning, so I enter the workday energized. Before I do anything for anyone else, I work for myself.

When dealing with a fear of missing out, determine the actual loss. That will need you to consider if the consequence of making a mistake is greater than the consequence of doing nothing. This decision is getting out of the weeds and is called leadership. It is moving from task level to considering organizational level.

Likely, the people who work for you cannot do tasks as well as you can. There is a reason you are in your current position. It would be best if you focused on helping them improve to do the job well enough, allowing you to do other things like focus on your goals.

To execute your plan, you do need to evaluate the risk. Do not lose sight of the obligations that you need to attend, such as family, bills, housing and food. You need to support your basic needs while you are achieving your goals.

My goal is to be an author. I have to maintain a house, support a family, including college tuition and many other obligations. Financially, I can not afford to stop everything and start writing. That is why I am up at 5:00 AM drinking coffee and writing while watching the news.

I see the risks that would come with jumping in at the deep end. I chose a dual path, my regular duties and my goals. Dual paths are a lot more work, but I have mitigated my risks.

The risks are not an excuse not to start; they are merely a measure of how you should start. If you have a two-income household, you may have more options. If you are worried about expenses, review your costs and reduce them wherever possible. Do you need premium cable and four streaming services?

Starting a business is risky. In your research and planning, you should have analyzed that risk.

One risk you will encounter is asymmetric information. Asymmetric information is when one party in a transaction has more information than the other party.

- Buying a car – the owner knows more about the car than you do.
- Interviewing for a job – you know more about yourself; the interviewer knows more about the company.
- Taking a class- you know the course description; the teacher knows the content.
- Getting married – you know you, your spouse knows themself.

Since you have the best understanding of the risks, it is time to mitigate (reduce or minimize) those risks. Most of this book discussed planning and mitigating your risks. You can't eliminate risks when you are working towards a challenging goal.

When you push yourself, there is always a chance you will fall. All the work and planning you've done has prepared you to overcome those risks , or if you do fall, to cushion your landing.

No matter what you do, there is a risk. Part of working toward a big goal is accepting that risk. If you challenge yourself, there is a chance you will fail, but failing does not make you a failure. If you never fail, you are not setting big enough goals.

Once you accept that it is okay to fail, you will feel a sense of freedom. We tend to put ourselves in a cage built on what other people think, the fear of failure, and over-planning. The cage can feel comforting. You feel protected in the cage as no one can touch you in there. It is too easy to stay there.

The cage can be:

- a job you hate.
- a bad relationship.
- working on other people's goal at te expense of yours.

The cage gives you a false sense of security and keeps you from growing. Let's liken this to the analogy of a lobster growing. The lobster has a shell that protects it but limits its growth. It is very similar to the cage. If the lobster wants to grow, it needs to molt, lose its shell, and grow a new one. The lobster's molting is similar to our process of growth. The lobster finds a place that is safe from predators. We mitigate our risks and build our support teams. The lobster sheds its shell and grows a new one. We execute our plan. Once the shell is hard, the lobster goes back into the world, as do we when working toward our goals. If you are in the cage, you are the first mouse. You need to get out of the trap if you want the cheese!

The key to execution is getting over the fear. "Courage is not the absence of fear, but rather the assessment that something else is more important than fear."

— FRANKLIN D. ROOSEVELT

Is your goal more motivating than your fear? We all have insecurities. We are afraid of what people will think of us. We are afraid of disappointing ourselves or our families. We are afraid that we will lose our stuff, our standing and our people's love.

When you take an honest look at the risks you encounter and planning and building your teams, you will find that the potential losses are not as bad as you think.

I have had some significant failures in my career. I have had setbacks and made screw-ups, but I am still here. I can look back and obsess on things I've done wrong in the past and dwell on should-haves.

- I should have taken that job.
- I shouldn't have quit that job.
- I should have focused more on getting ahead.
- I should have lost weight when I was younger.

I have obsessed and still obsess about these things. Negative self-talk just pops into our heads, and that never stops. Some of us have a more difficult time battling to control it than others. For whatever reason, negative self-talk plagues me. There are days I need to physically and mentally force myself to action.

I have learned from all of my should-haves that action cures doubt and is the only way to achieve goals. When I reflect on my past, I see that most regrets come from things not done. Dwelling in inaction is like the lobster trying to grow but refusing to shed its shell. It outgrows its skin.

Think about a job in which you spent too much time. You know that you can do more, but the company has pigeonholed you for whatever reason. You feel bigger than your job and tremendous pressure that you need to grow. By not acting on it, you come to a point where your shell pops. You get fired, you have health issues and your relationships suffer. It is like a lobster that molts in the open and is vulnerable to predators.

If your fears rule you, you will become bitter, causing you to head into a downward spiral.

You have to make sure that when you are working that you are actually working. When you get nervous, you may find yourself reverting to the planning stage, at the expense of working toward your goals. You focus on plans and avoid working toward your goals.

Setting goals is an exciting time. You see what you can accomplish, and you get excited about the future. Planning is an integral part of success. It is also a trap. You can get so wrapped up in preparation that you never execute your plans. You get stuck in a couple of areas:

1. The fear of missing something.
2. Lack of execution.

Don't let the fear of missing out drive your decisions.

When you are planning, you are working with limited information. You cannot predict the future, so you need to make assumptions. These assumptions are best if you base them on experience and a broad knowledge base, but they are still assumptions. You need to plan with the best information you have and not get trapped in a discussion whirlpool where you talk yourself in circles and never come to a conclusion.

Have a greater propensity for action than discussion

The time comes when you need to stop planning and start working. Ideas do not bring results; actions from ideas bring results. Set milestones for your planning time, and when that is complete, start doing. You will never achieve your goals by sitting in a conference room talking about plans. You need to take action.

Remember that plans are written on paper, not carved in stone. As you are working, you can review your progress and determine how your plans are working toward achieving your goals. If they are not working, YOU CAN CHANGE THEM!

Action is vital to achieving goals. Sitting in the conference room talking about doing things is comfortable; you dwell in the warmth of the potential, thinking about all the great things you can do, and you feel good.

Going into the cold, unpredictable world of action can be scary and stressful, but you need to enter this world to succeed. Action leads to results!

You may think that this story is extreme but think about your own goals. How many times have you pushed the start of your fitness plan to "next Monday"? We have all dwelt in planning and avoided action with statements like "I will achieve "FILL IN THE BLANK" after "SOME ARTIFICIAL DEADLINE.""

At some point, planning needs to end. Take action and achieve your goals!

Action can be the impetus to achieving your goals. Just as every journey starts with one step, every achievement begins with one move. When you feel stuck in the mud, do something.

- Hate your job? Update your resume. Apply for another job.
- Want to write a book – write an outline – write every day.
- Want to fix your house? – paint one room.

Whatever your goals, break your plan into digestible parts and start working. Thinking about getting out of the mud and achieving goals reminds me of the holiday special, A Year Without a Santa Claus. The Winter Warlock was afraid to move forward, and Chris Kringle showed him how to put one foot in front of the other. The same happens in your journey to achieve your goals; you put one foot in front of the other, and soon you'll be walking across the floor.

You can achieve your goals. You know what success means to you. You set goals based on your definition of success. You are using your mind to learn what you need. You are taking care of your body, so you have the energy. You manage your personal brand so people see you as someone who can achieve goals. You build your team to have the support you need.

Go out and live your life based on your definition of success!

Set challenging goals; plan but be pragmatic; know your surroundings; keep calm and think things through; set milestones to mark your progress; persevere during the tough times; accomplish your goals; analyze what you did right and wrong. Now set your sights on bigger and better goals.

By setting milestones, you have a better chance of achieving your goals. There are fitness challenges, asking that you complete 5,000 repetitions of an exercise. Let's say that you choose pushups, and you have never done pushups before. If you try to do 50 pushups your first day, you will hurt yourself and get discouraged. You need to set achievable milestones and stick with them.

You can do a test run and figure you can do ten pushups. You do that for a week and add five. The following week you add more and follow the pattern. Your milestone is 70 pushups the first week and 105 the following, and 140 the next. As you hit milestones, you build skills and confidence. As your confidence grows, you will find that your most challenging obstacle is your mind and that it gives up before your body. With focus, you can increase your output and create more challenging milestones.

Your milestones act as encouragement and an accountability setter. As you hit milestones, you gain confidence propelling you forward to hit your goals. The milestones push you to act. If you have a goal of losing 50 pounds in four months, you can start next week. If you have a goal of losing three pounds this week, you need to start now.

Martial arts use belts as milestones, and this gets mixed reviews. Some say it shows accomplishments others feel it is a type of participation trophy. Either can be correct. I attended the martial arts schools with specific requirements, tests and evaluations to advance. I have witnessed some schools lax in their testing and passing students who did not make the mark.

What is the lesson here? You need to set your milestones. You need to be prepared and practice martial arts not until you get it right but until you no longer get it wrong. Set realistic milestones. Don't give yourself a pass because you tried; you need to hold yourself accountable. If you have a team, ask them to hold you accountable. In martial arts, I have people who look up to me. If I did not pass a test and accepted an unearned belt, I would disappoint them. When I am struggling and need a boost, I think of that. There were times my kids were present, and if they weren't, I think I would have quit. Having someone else holding you accountable will always help you.

You will give up on yourself before your team of trusted advisors gives up on you. That is a fundamental reason to have a team around you and hold you accountable.

Without the milestones and an accurate measuring mechanism, you are acting for the sake of action and not really moving toward your goal. You need to act with intent.

Do you know where you stand in your goals? Have you looked at your plan since you wrote it? Do you even know where you can find a copy?

It is vital to keep the plan out in front of you. How can you hold yourself accountable if you don't know your plan? Accountability does not just pop up at the end of the year. That accountability starts when you finalize the plan. Where you are in your plan should not be a surprise to you.

Setting goals can be as great of a feeling as accomplishing goals. You tend to get excited about beginnings and endings. In the planning sessions, you look to next year thinking "new year, new me" or whatever mantra is in style. You finish your planning sessions and have big roll-outs for your plans. On the other side, you have celebrations for achieving goals. You get a cake when you close a big sale, and we have a party when we reach that particular milestone. We are excited about the beginning and the end, but what about the middle? Do you know how you are doing along the way?

In the middle, you get so busy that you forget to evaluate your performance as you move along. This lack of evaluation can result in big surprises that can be problematic if they reveal you have done poorly. Regularly measuring progress is the key to avoiding surprises. Do you know where you stand with your goals?

Knowing where you stand when working toward your goal is your responsibility. There is no reason for surprises. To understand where you stand, you need to measure. As you start measuring progress, if you find that your goals aren't clear, you need to revisit your plan and resolve any issues. You should make sure the goals are clear and that you have enough information to achieve them. Reapply the OODA Loop to make sure you are on track.

To have the confidence to accomplish your goals, you need to know how to measure your performance appropriately. If you are a salesperson with a revenue target, you need to measure the revenue to gauge how much more you need to reach your objectives. If your target is the number of sales transactions, your measurement is incorrect if you gauge your performance against the revenue. You will have had a false sense of success, thinking you are doing well, and will be surprised at falling short of the applicable target.

As a manager, measuring is even more critical. You need to know not just where you stand but where your people stand. Their goals are your goals, and just as they will have to face you at the end of the year, you will need to face your boss. At the end of the year, the meetings will bring fewer surprises if everyone understands the importance of the measurements from the outset.

Regular measurement of progress gives you a better chance of reaching your goals. The only guaranteed way to know if your strategy is not working is to measure your results. You can't make course adjustments if you don't see that you are off course.

The purpose of planning is to achieve goals; it prevents you from just going through the motions. Without this focus and the measured action in the middle, your planning and round-up are just going through the motions. If you have not measured your results, start now. You will have the information you need to communicate with your manager and subordinates. It will indicate whether your plan is working or if you need to change your strategy to move forward, giving you a better chance of achieving your goals. Dust off that plan and start using it!

I want to see the people around me grow and achieve their goals. Those who don't want to put in the effort to change and enjoy the status quo also don't want to see you succeed. It is harder for them to blame their circumstances when everyone around them is growing. When you lead your movement, you will attract success-driven people. On the other side, you will also attract the anger of those who want to stay where they are.

Your existence threatens the status quo of people's self-talk and beliefs, causing them to want to drag you down. This reaction becomes tough to accept when you find one of your friends in that group. Having a strong team supporting you will get you through this criticism and potential drag on your progress.

Reflection

What is keeping you from starting your goals today? What are you going to do to fix it?

How are you going to use what you learned in this book to achieve your goals?

How will you measure your progress?

Looking at your past progress, are you still on track?

Are you still using the OODA Loop?

Are you ready to address any bumps in the road?

Pull out your journal. Are there any areas you need to review? Where do you need help? Use this book as a guide and consult experts.

Takeaways

You are responsible for your success. You need to act if you are going to achieve your goals.

You will never have all the information you need to make decisions.

You need to overcome the fear of missing out.

Your planning and work should give you the confidence to move forward.

- You have defined your definition of success.
- You have set goals based on that definition.
- You have analyzed the situation – using The OODA Loop.
- You have researched your goal – Mind.
- You are taking care of yourself, so you have the energy to succeed – Body.
- You can present yourself and your goal to attract people – Brand.
- You have surrounded yourself with people who want to succeed – Team.

Yes! You have built a powerful machine that can propel you forward and mitigate your risks. It will give you the best chance to succeed.

If you don't have a clear plan, go back to the relevant chapter and review it.

Your success depends on you. You have the tools; you have the desire. Put in the work and get the success you deserve!

Results

You have broken out of your cage. You are now in a better position to achieve your goals than ever before.

The path you are on is curvey and has its ups and downs, successes and failures, but if you stick with it, you will accomplish what you set out to do!

The power is within you! You have the tools. Put in the work, and you will achieve your goals!

NOTES

NOTES

NOTES